The Family of ‘Imrān

The Family of ʻImrān

A Commentary on Chapter 3: *Surat Al-ʻImrān*

Keys to the Qur'an
Volume 2

Shaykh Fadhlalla Haeri

Garnet Publishing

New Edition

Keys to the Qur'an 5 volume set ISBN 1 873938 05 5
Volume 1 *The Cow:* ISBN 1 873938 33 0
Volume 2 *The Family of 'Imran* ISBN 1 873938 34 9
Volume 3 *The Heart of the Qur'an* ISBN 1 873938 35 7
Volume 4 *Four Selected Chapters of the Qur'an* ISBN 1 873938 36 5
Volume 5 *The Last Section of the Qur'an* ISBN 1 873938 37 3

British Library Cataloguing-in-Publication Data.
A catalogue record for this book is available from the British Library.

Jacket Design by Miranda Harvey
Typeset by Monde, London
Production by Anna Watson
Printed in Great Britain by Baker Brothers, Pontefract

Published by Garnet Publishing Ltd,
8 Southern Court, South Street,
Reading RG1 4QS, UK.

Contents

ACKNOWLEDGEMENTS

This series began in 1981 as part of the teachings of the Holy Qur'an in the United States and Europe. Numerous people had helped and worked to realize the original editions of these commetaries.

Considerable editing and modifications were carried out by Muna H. Bilgrami. Aliya Haeri's dedication and loyalty was invaluable in coordinating and supervising both the first series as well as the present series. Contributors to the present edition include Batool Ispahany, Kays Abdul Karim Mohammed, Dr. Salah al-Habib, Luqman Ali, Hasan Jobanputra, Christopher Flint and Syed Muyhi al-Khateeb. Special thanks are due to Dr. Yaqub Zaki for reading through the texts and for his helpful suggestions. Without the encouragement and enthusiasm of Dr. Omar Hamza's love of the Qur'an, this present edition would not have been possible.

AUTHOR'S BIOGRAPHY

Shaykh Fadhlalla Haeri was born and raised in the ancient Holy City of Kerbala, Iraq, and was educated in Europe and the United States. His professional background included the founding of companies in the oil industry as well as in international business. The rediscovery of the full Islamic heritage of his birth and its prophetic perfection came about through an awakening to the inner meanings of its outer teachings and practices. Since the 1970's, Shaykh Haeri has taught the Qur'an extensively throughout his travels, both in the East and the West. He currently resides in England and continues to travel and lecture widely, and is the author of many books.

TRANSLITERATION

CONSONANTS

ا	*alif*		ض	*ḍād*	ḍ
ب	*bā'*	b	ط	*ṭā'*	ṭ
ت	*tā'*	t	ظ	*ẓā'*	ẓ
ث	*thā'*	th	ع	*'ayn*	'
ج	*jīm*	j	غ	*ghayn*	gh
ح	*ḥā'*	ḥ	ف	*fā'*	f
خ	*khā'*	kh	ق	*qāf*	q
د	*dāl*	d	ك	*kāf*	k
ذ	*dhāl*	dh	ل	*lām*	l
ر	*rā'*	r	م	*mīm*	m
ز	*zay*	z	ن	*nūn*	n
س	*sīn*	s	ه	*hā'*	h
ش	*shīn*	sh	و	*wāw*	w
ص	*ṣād*	ṣ	ى	*yā'*	y

(ء hamza ')

VOWELS

ا	ā	َ	*fatḥa*	a
و	ū	ُ	*ḍamma*	u
ى	ī	ِ	*kasra*	i

' = assimilated vowels

INTRODUCTION

The Qur'an was revealed in an instant, issuing forth from a realm beyond time. Its unfolding within the domain of time, however, occurred over a span of twenty-three years, for it was necessary for the message to be fully absorbed, integrated and applied existentially. The message was, and continues to be, that Allah is the Reality behind all that one witnesses. He is beyond description and beyond perception by the senses. He has Attributes, but nothing can be associated with Him. He can only be alluded to. We are therefore taught to talk about Allah only in terms of His Attributes, not of His Essence.

The Qur'an came as a complete revelation, as one unit in space, as one instant in time, like a bolt of lightning that hits the sleeper and stuns him into wakefulness. It descended as a stream of truth upon the heart of the Prophet Muhammad, peace and blessings be upon him, his family and his righteous Companions;* for the Muhammadan application of the truth of the Qur'an is the vital complement. To try to understand the Qur'an without the Prophet would have been comparable to an attempt to use a medical manual with no previous medical experience: the manual is of little use to one who has no training. To know the meaning of reality one must follow a particular path of application. Thus, Islam is based on both the Qur'an and the Prophetic way (*Sūnnah*, سُنَّة).

All the basic principles of knowledge are contained in this book. It is an existential guide for perpetual life. The message of the Qur'an is based on balance, on living a life which inevitably leads to a better future, materially and morally, both on an individual and a social level.

The purpose of the Qur'an is for its message to be absorbed

* It is customary, whenever the name of the Prophet Muhammad is mentioned, to involve the peace and blessings of Allah upon him, his family and his righteous companions.

by the hearts of men. If there is no impact, then the remedy is only palliative. Superficial use of the Qur'an may be likened to a person who, hearing that vitamins are useful for the body's health, takes some indiscriminately. The vitamins are likely to be of some benefit, but they would have been far more useful had he known his specific condition and the properties of the vitamins, how they interact and enhance each other as well as how they might occasionally counteract one another. With this knowledge he would have been able to benefit maximally by taking the correct type and dosage. We hope to approach and use the Qur'an in this way.

The ability to derive meaning and knowledge from the Qur'an depends upon having the correct approach, and a humble, pure intention to attain knowledge. The assumption that one already knows something can be a hindrance. Therefore, one must be bereft, recognizing one's poverty, ignorance, weakness and need for knowledge and transformation. To approach the Qur'an, the seeker must possess the right courtesy (*adab*, أدَب) which will serve as a key to awaken the knowledge of the Qur'an already contained within the heart.

Drawing from the Qur'an, penetrating into it, integrating it into one's life and thus learning from it, require both outer and inner courtesy (*adab*, أدَب). If we approach the Qur'an with courtesy and love, it will unfold to us its values.

To gain the blessings and mercy of Reality through this ultimate, complete and balanced book of wisdom, one must appreciate its historical context and the overall environmental and ecological situation at the time of its descent. This includes understanding the civilization and culture of the time and place of its revelation, and more specifically, the nature of the people and their nomadic values. The Arab nomads of the Prophet's time, like nomads in general, were highly sensitized to their environment, for they had little protection from it. Because of the extreme harshness of their environment, the Bedouin Arabs lived continually on the verge of mortal danger; they had therefore developed extremely alert, agile and intuitive minds which were highly attuned to everything around them. Furthermore, the nomadic system of the Bedouin people was in constant conflict with the civic system of the city dwellers. Whenever the nomadic and sedentary cultures met, conflict as well as renewal occurred.

The qualities most highly valued in nomadic cultures were nobility, courage and generosity. The people of the desert were self-reliant and fiercely independent. They would not bow to another human being. The leader emerged naturally, and was recognized because of his qualities and character. In this system it was likely that the next leader would come from the present leader's clan or be related to him. In nomadic culture, the home, or tent, of the tribal chief was always open, and yet it was customary for people not to go begging, so as not to demean themselves. Thus, generosity was naturally balanced with integrity, self-esteem and patience.

The Qur'an arose amidst the Arab culture and a simpler way of life than ours, but its universal message enlivened the hearts of diverse people, even during the Prophet's lifetime. It is helpful if we are aware of the environment in Mecca and Medina at the time of the Qur'anic revelation in order then to apply it to the social and cultural situation of our time, for the Qur'an is a guide book in an actual prescriptive sense.

The Muhammadan path, as it evolved over the course of time, is inextricably linked, step by step, to the revelation of the Qur'an. It began with the acknowledgement of the Oneness of God and it ended with the establishment of a very strong community in which individuals, having completely recognized the laws governing human relationships, interacted in a manner that allowed each one to develop spiritually to his or her full capacity. The righteous Companions followed their Prophet Muhammad and thereby became established in their knowledge of God.

The Prophet saw in everyone the highest possible potential to be awakened to the higher inner knowledges. He recognized in all situations, even those which appeared to other men as afflictive, nothing other than Allah's mercy and compassion. He had the ability to see the ignorance that veils the hearts of men and causes them to act incorrectly, and he acted with understanding towards them. He worked to purify men's hearts, to help them evolve towards awakening to the inner life.

The few Muslims who were with the Prophet in the beginning were constantly subjected to oppression and opposition. The Prophet, wanting to save his small group of original followers, recommended that many travel to a place of safety, since living in Mecca had become impossible; for as their numbers grew so did opposition to them. The atmosphere had become increasingly polarized and hostile. The Muhammadan light, translated into a code of conduct, had become a major threat to the tribal habits of a people who took fierce pride in their ancestral ways. Their factional loyalties often led them to resort to brute force, with total disregard for logic, reason and human values. This polar-ization in Mecca would lead inevitably to violence.

In contrast to the clans in Mecca, some of the people of Medina saw light and usefulness in the message of Islam. Whereas the people of Mecca regarded the Prophet as no more than the son of one of their own kind, and could not accept his prophethood, the people of Medina, an agrarian people who were settled and more receptive, welcomed the Prophet and his followers, who upon arrival immediately began to build a mosque and homes: they embarked upon creating a community. But with a community also came problems: 'Surely We have created man in affliction' (90: 4).

The Family of 'Imrān (*Surat al 'Imrān*) was revealed mostly around the second or third year after the migration to Medina, although certain passages came somewhat later. Its dating has been deduced from the references to events which occurred at that time, namely the Battle of Uḥud. A major part of the chapter deals with the topic of hypocrisy. If one looks into one's own heart, one will occasionally witness how deep and subtle hypocrisy can be. An important lesson in The Family of 'Imrān is how to break free from the veil of hypocrisy.

The Battle of Uḥud, the second major battle between the young Muslim community and the Quraysh of Mecca, revealed a wide range of human weaknesses amongst the followers of the Messenger Muhammad. Curiously, the word *Uḥud* (أُحُد) is linguistically connected to *Aḥad* (أَحَد), which is a Divine Attribute meaning 'the One'. *Uḥud* thus could imply a comprehensive exposition of divine unity which takes place on the battlefield. In truth every moment is *Uḥud*, but we generally escape to relative short-term safety, unaware that eventually we must face the enemy. 'With your Lord alone on that day shall be the place of rest' (75: 12). There is no escape. 'Whither to fly ?' (75: 10); and, 'O man, surely you must strive hard toward your Lord until you meet Him' (84: 6). By what power and grace can one possibly escape?

It is up to us to perceive the plot of the One (*Aḥad*, أَحَد) which was exemplified during the era of the Prophet at the Battle of Uḥud. We need to delve into its meaning and grasp its truth, for much of what appears to be real is nothing but illusion, and the more we pursue illusions the more we are confused. The truth is that everything emanates from one source and returns to it. Life in this world pushes, pulls, encourages and entices us towards that source. This is the meaning of Allah's mercy and the perfection of His natural laws. Multiple manifestations all emanate from One Essence.

To behave with propriety towards the Creator, we must behave with propriety towards ourselves. But in order to check and balance oneself until that fine point of deep propriety is reached, we need to attain a state of spontaneous awareness. For this it is necessary to follow the example of others who have reached the goal, like tuning a musical instrument to the correct pitch using a tuning fork.

To discover subtle hypocrisy one need only look into one's own heart. There, within the self, one will find all the contradictions of conflict and duality. Yet out of this torment one can reach enlightenment: a person who has not experienced internal conflict is unlikely to be awakened to the knowledge of, and adherence to, the source of harmony within.

The commentary on The Family of 'Imrān contained within this volume differs from the traditional approach of Qur'anic commentators, for we intend to share its eternal values and its constant applicability within the deep realm of truth. Towards this end, much of the historical background which is widely available has not been included. However, where historical information is necessary to help illuminate the verse, it has been referred to.

We will examine the linguistic roots of numerous key terms so as to highlight their different facets as well as their specific meanings in the context in which they are used. We will allow ourselves to roam through the incredibly rich, delightful garden of communication and transformation, it is to be hoped within properly observed boundaries.

THE FAMILY OF 'IMRĀN

Chapter 3: *Surat Al-'Imrān*

بِسْمِ اللهِ الرَّحْمَٰنِ الرَّحِيمِ

In the Name of Allah, the Beneficent, the Merciful.

الٓمٓ

1 **Alīf Lām Mīm.**

Just as creation appears to have a physical structure, so does the Qur'an. From non-existence the letters come into being by a stroke of the pen. The letters are the foundation of the words which make up its sentences and thus impart meaning, just as the variegated forms of creation are contained within various systems that also provide meaning. From the One comes an infinite number of creational possibilities which indicate their truly infinite and unfathomable Source.

اللهُ لَآ إِلَٰهَ إِلَّا هُوَ الْحَيُّ الْقَيُّومُ

2 **Allah, [there is] no god but He, the Living, the Self-Subsisting by Whom all things subsist.**

The chapter begins by affirming what is most important in creation, namely (*tawḥīd,* تَوْحِيد), that is, unity, the Oneness of Allah. The Qur'an asserts that there is only one Creator from whom creation emerges. The most exalted definition and highest description of this Creator is that He has no other partner. There is no deity but Allah, the Absolute Creator.

Another description of Allah is that He is forever sentient or living. How can we experience life and death unless there is an immutable foundation, forever holding both in Its grasp. How is it that we are alive? We must be deriving life as well as all our other attributes (singular *sifah*, صِفَة) from a Reality which contains all these attributes. The reason that man seeks to prolong his life unnaturally is, in fact, because he is worshipping – albeit misguidedly – the Everlasting Who is within us. All attributes are from Allah, through whose grace everyone is constantly given the opportunity of knowledge and awakening. The Qur'an says, 'All that is in the heavens and the earth glorify Allah, the Sovereign King, the Sacred, the Mighty, the Wise' (62: 1).

Every created entity in this existence is glorifying, worshipping and adoring the Attributes of Allah, the Controller of all. Everyone wants to possess these Attributes, because man desires Allah; yet we already have Allah, we are already in the embrace of Allah. There is no escape from that One Reality; there is no escape from the laws of Allah which are the manifestation in creation of His Attributes.

It is up to us to experience His laws, not in a dualistic or fragmentary fashion, but as a totality, until we see nothing but Allah manifesting Himself through His different Attributes. If a particular event seems to be incongruous, we need only reflect upon its cause to understand it. If the event conforms to its context, then it has followed His laws. If we were to think, hear and see correctly and naturally, then everything around us would be coherent. Whatever appeared incomprehensible, once examined, would reveal its inner meaning.

Every cause has an effect, and every effect stems from a cause, except for the One-and-Only Source, Allah. Allah is Self-Subsisting, beyond cause and effect. Everything except Allah falls within laws that can be understood. All of creation emanates from a root, from a cause that encompasses and controls it all without being tarnished, touched or affected by it. This is the puzzle into which we are born, and we are given our entire lifetime to solve it. Its solution is its dissolution.

By submitting and dissolving the self into the truth that lies within, we unify our actions and intentions fully. Then we will find that every experience is covered by the mercy of Allah, thereby deepening our faith along the path. By this faith our certainty will be increased, and we will be led to the realization that this life is an emanation indicating its source and its natural return to it. Life then becomes an experience to be valued and respected, because one respects the Giver of the experience. Life is not acceptable unless it is put experientially into the right perspective. Life is only a training-ground where man may come to know the meaning of the words, 'Allah, there is no god but Him, the Living, the Self-Subsisting, by Whom all things subsist.'

نَزَّلَ عَلَيْكَ الْكِتَابَ بِالْحَقِّ مُصَدِّقًا لِّمَا بَيْنَ يَدَيْهِ
وَأَنزَلَ التَّوْرَاةَ وَالْإِنجِيلَ

3 **He has truthfully revealed the Book to you, verifying that which came before; and He revealed the Torah and the Gospel.**

In this verse the Prophet Muhammad and all who truly follow him are addressed by Allah. The Qur'an as revealed to Muhammad confirms the truth of the earlier books of the Torah and the Gospels. The message of these divinely inspired Books is from the same One Source, but revealed at different times, for different civilizations or cultures. The books of Moses and Jesus were adequate for their time, and the teachings of Jesus superseded what remained of the oral Talmudic tradition.

The Qur'an of Muhammad supersedes all previous revealed teachings. It is the final message, as it encompasses the collective prophetic consciousness. The Arabic language of the Qur'an and the continuous chain of transmission of its teachings ensures its authenticity and safeguards it. Attempts to interpret the Qur'an and the Prophetic path in order to justify a personal prejudice, or wrongly to reinforce unjust actions, continue. Despite this, Islam remains preserved as it was originally and the behaviour of Muslims can always be judged against it by whoever has been given its light.

مِن قَبْلُ هُدًى لِّلنَّاسِ وَأَنزَلَ الْفُرْقَانَ ۗ إِنَّ الَّذِينَ كَفَرُوا بِآيَاتِ
اللَّهِ لَهُمْ عَذَابٌ شَدِيدٌ ۗ وَاللَّهُ عَزِيزٌ ذُو انتِقَامٍ

4 **Aforetime, a guidance for mankind, and He revealed the Discrimination. Surely, those who disbelieve in the revelations of Allah shall suffer a severe punishment. And Allah is Mighty, the Lord of Retribution.**

The Qur'an has several names, two of which are 'The Book' (*al-Kitāb*, الكِتَاب) and 'The Discrimination' (*al-Furqān*, الفُرْقَان). The Book of knowledge and understanding is based on discrimination, the differentiation between what is right and what is wrong. By reading this Book, we learn to differentiate between truth and falsehood, transience and permanence.

What is emphasized in this verse is that the knowledge of Allah is the highest priority. Whoever denies the signs of Allah, whoever denies the proof of the existence of the Creator, whoever denies the interconnectedness of everything in this creation, whoever denies the one power from which stem different manifestations and apparently opposing values or attributes, is in a state of affliction and pain, that is, 'severe punishment' (*'adhāb shadīd*, عَذَاب شَدِيد). Ignorance underlies all pain. Once the reason behind the outcome of a given situation is known, immediate relief and comfort are found, though the difficulty of the situation may not yet be resolved. Through thorough knowledge of any situation, acceptance becomes possible, and with this acceptance positive, successful action can be undertaken.

Understanding and acceptance are aspects of discrimination, of recognizing what is what. If one fails to see the one thread behind the many woven patterns, the result is continual suffering, difficulty and affliction.

إِنَّ اللَّهَ لَا يَخْفَىٰ عَلَيْهِ شَيْءٌ فِي الْأَرْضِ وَلَا فِي السَّمَاءِ

5 **Surely nothing in the earth or in the heavens is hidden from Allah.**

The Living, Self-Subsistent Reality (*al-Ḥayy al-Qayyūm,* الحيّ القيّوم) is also the All-Hearing, All-Seeing and All-Knowing Reality. Nothing is hidden from Allah. Where can one turn that Allah and His manifestations do not exist? Where can one hide from that which gives one life? Wherever one goes, one's life-support system is already there. How can one say that one has no knowledge of Allah– for where is it that Allah is not? The answer is truly that such a place does not exist. Anyone who recognizes this fact knows that wherever one turns there is the face of Allah. If man is at all times aware that Allah sees what is in his heart, he will naturally labour to purify his heart. He will seek to reveal what is in it so that it might thereby be rendered wholesome and pleasing to Allah, for there is nothing more purifying than revealing one's heart to someone who is willing to listen.

The hypocrisy (*nifāq,* نفَاق) of one who knows that nothing is hidden from Allah will evaporate by continual exposure to air and light. The Arabic verbal root from which the word for hypocrite springs means 'to tunnel'. Like a mole in a tunnel the hypocrite cannot be easily caught, because the tunnel has more than one exit hole. It is a secret underground tunnel which one may enter by one hole and come out through another. One is always justifying one's prejudices and veils – never catching the self out. By recognizing that Allah knows everything, the labyrinth is unearthed. A technique for reducing hypocrisy is to think of one's heart, one's inner thoughts and motivations as exposed. In truth, every cell within a man reflects his true intentions. Nothing in the heavens or on the earth is hidden from the Reality which encompasses them both, and yet is beyond them.

هُوَ الَّذِي يُصَوِّرُكُمْ فِي الْأَرْحَامِ كَيْفَ يَشَاءُ ۚ
لَا إِلَٰهَ إِلَّا هُوَ الْعَزِيزُ الْحَكِيمُ

6 **He shapes you in the womb as He pleases; there is no god but He, the Mighty, the Wise.**

Man himself is a form, a picture (*ṣūrah*, صُورَة), a representative of Reality. He is an example of Reality, because he encompasses within himself the meaning of everything that he experiences; he is a microcosm of creation. If man did not contain within himself the potential to understand everything outside himself, how then could he understand the external world? There is within us a microworld which enables us to reflect the macroworld outside. This is how He has 'shaped you in the womb'. The Arabic verbal root for 'wombs' (*arḥām*, أَرْحَام) means 'to be merciful or compassionate' (*raḥima*, رَحِمَ). The womb with its function of propagation is a great manifestation and direct proof of Allah's ongoing mercy. The word for 'womb' also means 'relationship, kinship'. It is important for everyone to extend mercy and generosity to their family. The person who has embraced Islam, but whose family has not, should try to share his faith with his family, not by forcing it upon them, but by gentle words and guidance whenever possible. The enemy is not the family itself but the ignorance based on culture and habit that has been allowed to take hold over the family. It is actions that are evil, not people.

There are seven factors which affect the make-up of the individual. The first is to do with the character of one's parents: there is no doubt that one inherits physical and other characteristics from one's predecessors. Another factor is the act of conception itself; this relates to the love between the parents and the depth of their relationship. The third factor is the mother's diet and overall physical, mental, emotional and spiritual state while the child is developing in the womb. The fourth factor concerns the conditions at the moment of birth; the way in which this transition occurs is critical. To be born under the glaring lights of a hospital operating theatre, surrounded by unknown people who are preoccupied with their own problems, is not the best way to enter life. Traditionally, in the past, children were born at home, where the mother was at ease in her own environment, with her own people who treated her lovingly. The fifth factor is the child's treatment during the first two years, including the diet, love, attention and warmth that the mother gives it, the love that exists between both the parents and the baby. The sixth element is the child's upbringing, grooming and social environment. A child who is brought up in a criminal environment is more likely to take to crime, while one brought up in an environment of love, honesty and harmony is more likely to repeat aspects of the same pattern.

The seventh factor is the most important one: a person's power of will and clarity of objective in life. One may have inherited genetically certain weaknesses or physical handicaps or been born into a deprived or criminal environment. One may be aware of all this and yet have the strength and determination to go through life, overcoming the past and rising above those limitations.

Man is like a holographic image: he is potentially a reflection of Reality, if he chooses to be. A holograph is an image produced on a photosensitive plate through the use of a laser beam; a holographic image not only reflects the object from which it is made, but it also behaves as if it were the object itself. The degree to which man can reflect the highest Reality is as accurate as the degree of his willingness to submit, surrender and be committed to Allah.

هُوَ الَّذِي أَنزَلَ عَلَيْكَ الْكِتَابَ مِنْهُ آيَاتٌ مُّحْكَمَاتٌ هُنَّ أُمُّ الْكِتَابِ
وَأُخَرُ مُتَشَابِهَاتٌ ۖ فَأَمَّا الَّذِينَ فِي قُلُوبِهِمْ زَيْغٌ فَيَتَّبِعُونَ مَا تَشَابَهَ مِنْهُ
ابْتِغَاءَ الْفِتْنَةِ وَابْتِغَاءَ تَأْوِيلِهِ ۗ وَمَا يَعْلَمُ تَأْوِيلَهُ إِلَّا اللَّهُ ۗ
وَالرَّاسِخُونَ فِي الْعِلْمِ يَقُولُونَ آمَنَّا بِهِ كُلٌّ مِّنْ عِندِ
رَبِّنَا ۗ وَمَا يَذَّكَّرُ إِلَّا أُولُو الْأَلْبَابِ

7 **He it is Who has revealed the Book to you in which are decisively clear verses, the basis of the Book; others are allegorical. Those whose hearts are distorted follow the part which is allegorical, seeking dissension, and seeking to give it [their own] interpretation; but none knows its interpretation except Allah. And those who are firmly rooted in knowledge say: We believe in it, it is all from our Lord. None remind except those who have innermost understanding.**

If the Qur'an is regarded as a whole, there is no obscurity in its allegories or doctrine. The Qur'an is the clear book in which there is no doubt; doubt exists only in the minds of men because of their veils of ignorance.

The word 'basis' (*umm*, أُمّ) also means 'mother', implying that these verses are the source or foundation of the Book. Mecca was called 'the mother of villages' (*umm al-qurā*, أُمّ القُرى), because it was a trading centre. A closely related word in the Qur'an means 'unlettered' (plural *ummīyīn*,أميين), meaning those who have not had a book, in particular the people of Mecca before Islam. It also refers to the inability of most of the Arabs of that time to read and write.

Unlettered also means not formally taught, for the Prophet, according to tradition, had not been taught to read or write at the time the revelations of the Qur'an began. It is known that the Prophet spoke numerous dialects and understood foreign languages, and encouraged the teaching of reading and writing. Many prisoners captured by the Muslims in battle were offered the opportunity of gaining their freedom by teaching the Muslims to read and write. It is said that in each of the nine mosques of Medina there was at all times someone available to teach people to read and write.

'Those whose hearts are distorted' deviate by turning away from Reality. Through knowledge one sees that there is no turning away from the path of Allah, for there is no other way. Man has come from Allah, he is sustained by the grace of Allah, and he is returning to that everlasting Source. If the heart is not completely at one with Reality, it will remain confused. If the heart is not fused to that awareness then it becomes confused.

People who study the Qur'an without the correct courtesy of humility and openness of heart will not derive benefit. They see only what is doubtful, which increases their own confusion. They are 'seeking dissension', because they are subject to temptations which cause distraction. If man recognizes what has confused him, he is able to avoid it the next time he is confronted by a similar situation.

There is no dispute or doubt about the real way once one is fully on that path. The Prophetic life-transaction (*dīn*, دين) is not open to discussion. Those who are true to Islam, who have surrendered to Reality, cannot be in discord. Dispute arises because of lack of accord, hence discord. A man who has submitted to Allah is in the hand of Allah, the hand of absolute justice. If someone has entered into an argument, it is because he did not possess full discernment or discrimination (*furqān*, فُرْقَان) in the situation. Islam is truly the house of peace based on love and justice. It is at peace with its inhabitants and at war with those in ignorance and those who deny Allah.

Those whose hearts are wandering will cause distraction, confusion and dissension 'by seeking to give it their own interpretation (*ta'wil*, تأويل)'. They talk according to their own whims, 'but none knows its interpretation except Allah'. No one knows the roots of a thing except He who puts forth the roots and 'those who are firmly rooted in knowledge'. The ones who are firmly rooted in their trust in Allah will come to know more and more about the meanings of the manifestations of Reality. All power, actions and attributes come from the Lord and Sustainer. His mercy pervades all creation.

Knowledge and wisdom are but the beautiful and subtle veils of a higher reality. They produce a greater state of awareness and deeper understanding. The Prophet has said, 'The leaders of guidance are among my progeny (*Ahl al-Bayt*, أهل البيت) and some of my Companions (*Ṣaḥābah*, صَحَابَة). He whose right actions are clear, whose tongue always speaks the truth, whose heart is straight, and who guards his stomach and his sexual urge is one who is firmly established in knowledge. These people were not confused or in doubt. Confusion is a result of one's ignorance of cause and effect and the inconsistent relationship between intention and action. The confused person can only blame himself, seek knowledge and then take refuge in patience.

When Umm Salamah heard the Prophet repeat the supplication, 'O Lord Who turns the heart, establish my heart in Your way (*dīn*, دين)', she asked, 'O Messenger of Allah, will the hearts turn again ?' 'Yes,' he said, 'Allah has not created man from the children of Adam but that his heart is between His two fingers. If He wills He makes it straight and if He wills He makes it deviate.' Man cannot be arrogant about his faith (*īmān*, إيمان). One can never claim that one knows (for higher knowledge is limitless), or that one's knowledge is complete. Allah says, 'But none feels secure from Allah's plot [i.e. subtle ways], except those who are at a loss' (7: 99). Man must be constantly vigilant and diligent. The worst situation is to gain a little knowledge and then to feel arrogantly secure.

All that we experience comes from 'our Lord' (*Rabbanā*, رَبَّنَا). The Lord is that entity which brings us up to our full potential. A related word from the same root word as Lord means 'upbringing, education, edification' (*tarbīyah*, تَرْبِيَة), but there is no equivalent word for 'lord' in the English language that can adequately convey the idea of nurturing, and the process of gaining wisdom and fulfilment through being fostered and guided by Allah's Attribute of Lordship.

'None remind except those who have innermost understanding.' The word for 'innermost understanding' (*lubb*, لُبّ), also means 'essence, core', or 'reasoning mind'. Sometimes it connotes an understanding connected to the heart, but in the case of this verse it has the further connotation of achievement. The ability to remind depends on the ability to remember, to recall the original sub-genetic information that man is dependent upon Allah, Who has created out of love. If man is continually concerned about external manifestations in the realm of duality, he cannot reflect upon the One Source. The inner meaning of all our activities in life relates to discovering this truth, through surrender and understanding.

In the Qur'an some verses are absolutely clear and some are allegorical, appearing to be obscure. Qur'anic commentators often conjecture as to whether certain verses are allegorical or not. When the Qur'an is examined as a whole there is no obscurity; there is metaphor and symbolism, but there is no obscurity: 'These are the verses of the Qur'an, the verses of a clear book' (27: 1). The leaders of the Prophetic House related that 'the understanding of the Qur'an is by the Qur'an, because parts of the Qur'an explain other parts'. The Qur'an is complete unto itself and contains the entirety of meaning within itself.

Allah tells us that the clear verses are the basis of the book. What is allegorical or obscure may be understood in the light of what is clarified elsewhere. As we stated earlier, the word for 'basis' also means 'mother' as well as 'source, origin, foundation, essence, matrix'. A closely related word means 'one who remains in the natural condition of his surroundings'. This word came to refer to the Arabs in particular, and because they did not read or write, it came by extension to mean 'unlettered'. When this word was used in the Qur'an (7: 157) to describe the Prophet Muhammad, the ordinary meaning was that he was not taught in any formal sense, but that he had a natural connection to life and its source, and had therefore a primal, natural ability to 'read'. The Qur'anic description of 'unlettered' also emphasizes that the Prophet was not formally educated, but that his authority was based upon revealed knowledge.

One of the meanings of the Arabic word translated in this verse as 'interpretation' (*ta'wīl,* تأويل) is 'opinion.' If, for example, on a cloudy day someone comments that it is a good day, he probably means that in his opinion the day will be full of benefit. The listener, on the other hand, may interpret what he said as sarcastic, because the sky is obviously overcast. The first person might then say to the listener he has misinterpreted the speaker's words, (*awwalta kalāmī,* أوّلت كلامي), implying that the listener has read into them what he wanted to hear. Personal opinions regarding the meanings of the Qur'an must be guarded against. Some of the verses do not allow for interpretation while others lend themselves to a great number of meanings, both broad as well as deep. There are many pitfalls in interpreting according to one's own opinion.

An explicit example of a clear verse is, 'O you who believe, fasting is prescribed for you as it was prescribed for those before you, so that perhaps you may guard yourselves with fearful awareness' (2: 186). There is no doubt about the interpretation of this verse, nor room for different opinions about its meaning. An example of an allegorical verse is, 'Looking toward their Lord' (75: 23). One may ask how this is possible, for Allah cannot be seen, as He established with Moses: 'You will never see Me' (7: 143). The intellect allows one to understand that 'seeing Allah' refers to knowledge of Allah. The latter verse forces one to look deeply into the meaning of 'looking towards' in the former verse thereby finding that it also means 'directing one's attention towards'. Prophetic traditions may also be used to reinforce the understanding of the Qur'an. In this case a famous sacred tradition relates, 'The eyes cannot see Me, but the heart of the believing slave sees Me.'

Many verses that use worldly or linguistic terms are inadvertently given a physical interpretation. For example, the word for 'throne' (*'arsh,* عَرْش) in the verse, 'Then He [Allah] established himself on the throne' (*Thumma istawā 'alā al-'arsh,* ثُمَّ اسْتَوَى عَلَى العَرْش, 10: 3). The mind conjures up a giant-like being acting as puppeteer for the whole world, seated on an enormous throne. If we delve into the meaning of the Arabic word for 'throne' we will find that it means 'that upon which everything rests', indicating a foundation. Another example, mentioned many times in the Qur'an, is that Allah possesses all riches. Because man treasures his own insignificant trinkets, he may imagine an enormous treasure box, full of Allah's glittering treasures. In reality, however, Allah's treasures comprise the entire creation, comprising that which man comprehends as well as what he cannot comprehend.

There is a story related about an inquirer who asked Imam Ja'far al-Ṣādiq to explain a certain verse on three different occasions. Each time he received a different answer. Finally he queried the Imam about the differing interpretations and the Imam answered him thus: 'O Jābir, the Qur'an has an inner lining, and for that inner lining there is another inner lining, and for that inner there is another inner and yet another. O Jābir, there is nothing further from the intellect of man than the interpretation of the Qur'an.' Ja'far al-Ṣadiq's explanation illustrates that many verses can be interpreted from different angles and in subtle ways. While all of the interpretations are correct, at the same time care must be exercised so that one's opinion does not conceal a true reflection of the universality of the verse.

The entire Qur'an is a continuous exposition of the different facets of Reality. In a sense it is like man's life, the beginning, middle and end of which may be very different, yet interconnected. Likewise, the lives of individuals may appear to be radically different, but if we look at this multiplicity as a manifestation of a reality that has unchanging boundaries, we find written therein decrees which cannot be changed, decrees such as birth and death. There is a limit to the freedom we can exercise because of the natural boundaries that have been determined.

How can man comprehend his cause except by allegory (*mithal*, مِثَال) and deep reflection which results in the remembrance of his origin? The Qur'an is not meant to confuse us, but a person whose heart is not clear reflects the confusion contained therein. A man or woman of Allah does not see anything other than clarity in the Qur'an. If there are areas within it which are not understood, it could be that either the verse has been abrogated or that it contains an unfamiliar aspect of divine law. It could also be unclear because it requires more reflection before the various meanings interconnect.

Clear understanding of certain parts is the foundation for wider understanding: it is by means of light that we can distinguish shades of light. The way to approach the Qur'an is to take from it what is understandable and put it to use; if this is not done, one will not progress. If one fails to transfer the teachings into physical action, then our approach to the Book is faulty and we will be further deprived of knowledge.

رَبَّنَا لَا تُزِغْ قُلُوبَنَا بَعْدَ إِذْ هَدَيْتَنَا وَهَبْ لَنَا
مِن لَّدُنكَ رَحْمَةً إِنَّكَ أَنتَ الْوَهَّابُ

8 **Our Lord, do not allow our hearts to deviate after You have guided us, and grant us mercy from your Presence. Surely, You are the Generous Bestower.**

People who have tasted the sweetness of faith pray to their Lord and Sustainer for their hearts to be guided. Having tasted this sweetness and having seen the light of guidance (*hudā*, هُدى), they guard themselves. Their prayers are a reflection of their intention to protect themselves and keep their hearts safe. They beseech their Lord not to let them be misguided after they have seen the mercy (*raḥmah*, رَحْمة) of guidance, for they recognize this guidance as a gift from Allah, which, if lost, can never be replaced.

رَبَّنَا إِنَّكَ جَامِعُ النَّاسِ لِيَوْمٍ لَا رَيْبَ فِيهِ إِنَّ اللَّهَ لَا يُخْلِفُ الْمِيعَادَ

9 **Our Lord, surely You are the Gatherer of mankind on a day about which there is no doubt. Most certainly Allah will not fail to keep [His] promise of the appointed time.**

The people of faith have no doubt about the signs of Allah, nor do they give in to their whims. By remembering the Day of Reckoning, they remain aware at all times of the transient nature of this life. Remembrance of death is a means to freedom from the veils of the self and from constant justification of one's habitual actions. It is quite natural for us to continue our past habits and find good reasons and explanations for us to do so. The self has the knack of justifying what it wants. Without going back to the source as a reference point, one will find a justification for any action. That reference point can only be activated if we are in submission to Allah and in a state of spontaneous awareness. If, while experiencing anger, suspicion, greed or confusion, one is able to shut everything out and go into total inner silence and submission, one would be able to improve one's actions. Neutralization from within will bring about a positive result in one's direction.

This verse relates to us that those who have faith (*īmān*, إيمان) and are established in knowledge (*rāsikhūn fī al-'ilm* , رَاسِخُون في العِلْم) constantly remember that they will be gathered up on the Day of Reckoning. A person who lives with such remembrance will live in a manner which is detached but still present, exposed to his Creator and open to judgement at all times. He will not be enslaved by the world, and its attachments or its attractions. He lives as a free man because he is a slave only to Allah.

إِنَّ الَّذِينَ كَفَرُوا لَن تُغْنِيَ عَنْهُمْ أَمْوَالُهُمْ وَلَا أَوْلَادُهُم
مِّنَ اللَّهِ شَيْئًا ۖ وَأُولَٰئِكَ هُمْ وَقُودُ النَّارِ

10 **The wealth and children of those who disbelieve will not avail them against Allah. They are fuel for the Fire.**

In direct opposition to the way of life led by those who believe is the way of life of those who deny Allah. They fail to recognize the profundity of death, and have little or no belief in the reckoning after death. Whoever denies that this creation has come from, is sustained by, and is accountable to one Creator, has no refuge in his wealth or in his offspring – he is 'fuel for the Fire' (*waqūd al-Nār,* وَقُود ألنَار). Man's entire experience in the outer world is subject to unstoppable change. Because of this, some seek security in material accumulation. Certainly, such accumulation may bring about a certain element of comfort or pleasure, but once a person succeeds in gathering material wealth, insecurity and problems from other quarters will creep in.

Our understanding, knowledge and behaviour is very much subject to the condition of our hearts. The more hardened the heart, the more mechanistic and uninspired our lives become.

كَدَأْبِ آلِ فِرْعَوْنَ وَالَّذِينَ مِن قَبْلِهِمْ
كَذَّبُوا بِآيَاتِنَا فَأَخَذَهُمُ اللَّهُ بِذُنُوبِهِمْ
وَاللَّهُ شَدِيدُ الْعِقَابِ

11 **Like the people of Pharaoh and those before them. They rejected Our Signs, so Allah destroyed them because of their wrong actions. And Allah is severe in requiting wrong action.**

The people of Pharaoh and those who came before them denied the supreme sovereignty of Allah. Every effect has its cause, and this effect in turn becomes the cause of another effect. Life's experiences are all interrelated in a network. The transgression and disbelief of these people and their abuse of physical power and wealth resulted in a natural punishment. Their diligence was directed only towards their materialistic pursuits, and though the level of their outer technology was very high, it nevertheless did not save them: their inner technology – spiritual enlightenment – was missing.

قُل لِّلَّذِينَ كَفَرُوا سَتُغْلَبُونَ وَتُحْشَرُونَ
إِلَىٰ جَهَنَّمَ وَبِئْسَ الْمِهَادُ

12 **Say to those who disbelieve: You shall be overcome and driven to Hell. What a miserable place of rest!**

Tell the people who deny that Allah pervades, prevails over and controls all, that if they do not pursue a life that leads to the acknowledgement of this truth, they will experience the torment and agitation of the Fire. There is no resting place within fire, which is the description of Hell. Those who have not awakened in this life will be very rudely awakened on the Day of Reckoning.

If one is not aware of one's own basic motives and actions, it is unlikely that one would be aware of Allah's justice in all situations. The term 'luck' really implies our lack of knowledge of all the parameters that determine a desirable outcome. When a person describes an occurrence as luck, it means that his or her individual path crossed favourably with an overall environmental direction, and this conjunction was conducive to bringing about the end which he or she desired. Bad luck is the reverse of this process. A person has a certain objective, but does not know all the factors at play in the situation; at a certain point there is a clash with powerful, unknown factors which are in opposition to the achievement of the desire. These factors prevail, the objective fails – and we call this bad luck! The more one is aware and has knowledge, the less one sees 'good luck' or 'bad luck'. Rather, one sees efficiency or inefficiency.

The ignorant seeks to protect his ego, and is both unwilling and unable to see the situation as it is. The person who does not know and knows that he does not know is far better off than the person who thinks he knows, because he is more open to knowledge.

A prophetic saying states, 'People are the enemy of what they do not know'. Man by nature loves knowledge (*'ilm,* عِلْم). The search for knowledge is a great motivating factor in life. Indeed, man loves the Attributes of Allah, and one of His main Attributes is the All-Knowing (*al-'Alīm,* العَلِيم). The egotistic and selfish person will gloss over his areas of ignorance rather than admit he does not possess knowledge. If one does not start with knowledge of one's own self and inner state then one has not yet begun the process of spiritual growth.

قَدْ كَانَ لَكُمْ آيَةٌ فِي فِئَتَيْنِ الْتَقَتَا فِئَةٌ تُقَاتِلُ
فِي سَبِيلِ اللَّهِ وَأُخْرَى كَافِرَةٌ يَرَوْنَهُمْ مِثْلَيْهِمْ
رَأْيَ الْعَيْنِ وَاللَّهُ يُؤَيِّدُ بِنَصْرِهِ مَنْ يَشَاءُ
إِنَّ فِي ذَٰلِكَ لَعِبْرَةً لِأُولِي الْأَبْصَارِ

13 **Indeed there was a sign for you in the two armies [which] encountered each other. One party was fighting in the way of Allah and the other was an unbelieving force who saw the former as twice as many as themselves. And Allah strengthens those whom He pleases with His aid. Surely, there is a lesson in this for those who have insight.**

The Qur'an moves back and forth in time, while its central message is timeless. It does not allow one to fall into the trap of historical perspective, for its truth is for all time.

The chapter of The Family of 'Imrān was revealed soon after the Battle of Uḥud, which occurred in the third year after the Migration (*Hijrah*, هِجْرَة) from Mecca to Medina. The Battle of Badr was still fresh in the minds of the people. Historical references estimate that the Prophet had 313 men with him at Badr and that they had eight swords, six shields and two horses. On the other hand, the enemy was estimated to number about a thousand, all on horseback. The Muslims were ill-equipped outwardly but well-equipped inwardly, trusting that this life was only one fleeting moment in the manifestation of eternity. Without being suicidal, they were not afraid of death: they were men of Allah and therefore unafraid of Allah's creation.

Of the two groups fighting, one was fighting for Allah's sake. The other group was made up of clans who imagined the Muslims were greater in number than they actually were. The courage and fearlessness of the Muslims caused them to appear far more numerous. The light of Allah will prevail with the people who serve the cause of Allah and who always strive to move towards higher values. This is 'a lesson for those who have insight'.

In the Qur'an Allah says that if one does good the reward will be doubled or multiplied even further, but if one does wrong, he will experience merely its equivalent amount in return. The natural phenomenon is that goodness increases and multiplies while evil begets an equal consequence.

Anything that is done outside the laws of nature and of what is permissible is transgression. *Shayṭān* (شَيْطَان, Satan) means one who is 'cast out,' or has 'exceeded the bounds' of Allah. In the garden, where there was no duality, Adam did not know what a lie was. When the *Shayṭān* arose to entice him, Adam assumed that his voice was true Reality and therefore believed him. He did not believe the *Shayṭān* to be an enemy, because the realm of opposites, of duality, had not yet arisen.

زُيِّنَ لِلنَّاسِ حُبُّ الشَّهَوَاتِ مِنَ النِّسَاءِ وَالْبَنِينَ
وَالْقَنَاطِيرِ الْمُقَنْطَرَةِ مِنَ الذَّهَبِ وَالْفِضَّةِ
وَالْخَيْلِ الْمُسَوَّمَةِ وَالْأَنْعَامِ وَالْحَرْثِ ذَٰلِكَ مَتَاعُ
الْحَيَوٰةِ الدُّنْيَا وَاللَّهُ عِنْدَهُ حُسْنُ الْمَآبِ

14 The love of desires, of women and sons, hoarded treasures of gold and silver, well-bred horses, live-stock and tilth, is made fair-seeming to mankind. This is provision for the life of the world, while with Allah is the more excellent abode.

This verse is a compelling statement about the nature of man. Worldly desires seem attractive in his eyes. Man naturally loves gold and silver because they are signs of wealth. Well-bred horses and tilth' were also signs of wealth in the Prophet's time. Nowadays, however, man's wealth is measured by pieces of paper or electronic numbers. The strongest desire in a normal man is for intimacy with a woman, because in that state he becomes almost mindless, or to put it another way, with her he can experience a selfless bliss. A similar state is attained by emptying the mind in meditation. It is understandable that when one's mind is disturbed one seeks a physical form of relief. Disturbed men often have a stronger sexual drive than those who are in inner peace, but eventually that disturbance may take them to a point where they become sexually impaired.

Recreation and play are necessary in life. The fact that we have been created in order to know the Creator and then die can be searing if contemplated unceasingly. Play should, however, be contained, otherwise man will only bring harm to himself and others. The boundary in the case of relationships between man and woman is a contract within which each party fulfils their part. She accords him authority in exchange for protection and support. A man's responsibilities are different from a woman's. If they were the same, then role confusion would ultimately dismantle the normal, primal family structure. Much of what we are experiencing with the troubled youth in the West today is a result of role confusion and the dilution or loss of traditional family values. The glamorous image of the working woman in the factory or office has been created to make available a cheap work-force and to increase material productivity. Family culture, meanwhile, has broken down. Today children come home from school to an empty house and a microwave oven, instead of to a mother and companionship. Is it any wonder that drugs, alcohol and sexual promiscuity are ravaging the youth of today? When the biological process of birth takes over within the woman, the man, if he is of noble disposition, understands, protects and loves her so that the child who comes into the world will be someone who will live a life worthy of Allah's highest creation.

The Prophet said, 'O people, you are in a house of truce.' In this short life war is being waged between right and wrong, between this life and the next. The intentions and resultant actions of each individual will decide the outcome. Therefore we live in a state of truce. When asked, the Prophet explained that in the house of truce people are informed about the news of the purpose of creation, and they are encouraged to cut themselves off from this world by weaning themselves away from their love for it.

Excessive love and attachment to worldly desires are the cause of enslavement. The cure is moderation and taking the middle road until the desires are fulfilled or have fallen away from one's heart. For example, man is not necessarily disrespectful to Allah because he loves gold, for it is a material which exists naturally in His creation and inherently possesses noble qualities. What is wrong with possessing gold is the danger of arrogance, power and deprivation of others that its hoarding and accumulation bring. 'Alī ibn Abī Ṭālib said, 'The one who is abstemious (*zāhid*, زَاهِد) is not one who owns nothing; rather, he is the one who is not owned by anything.' There is no merit in possessing nothing, but there is great merit in not being owned by anything.

Desire and attraction are natural phenomena which cannot be resisted. Every person wants to increase his or her wealth. If we are willing to reflect honestly upon our motives, then, through experience, we will recognize the affliction that results if our motives are not pure. If we use the provisions (*matā'*, مَتَاع) of this world as useful tools for this short journey, then we are likely to be spared the agony of separation from them. What matters is our intention rather than the action itself. Those who forget that there is an end to this world, and a life to come after it, are described elsewhere as follows: 'And the *Shayṭān* has made their deeds fair-seeming to them and thus turned them from the way' (27: 24). Allah also says, 'The evil of their actions is made fair-seeming to them; and Allah does not guide the unbelieving people' (9: 37). Actions have a way of justifying themselves; a person's ugly deeds may be small at first, but if unchecked, they will increase with each day.

Thus spiritual seekers often go to the desert, where life can be lived more frugally. When the need for clothing and food is less, one can turn one's attention away from the world more easily. In a cold climate, however, one is totally enslaved to the elements, and because outer protection and order must be established first, the outer prevails over the inner. Purification starts from the outer layer and works its way inwardly to the subtle core, until one finds that the outer and the inner are totally connected. One who has attained inner peace will naturally avoid situations which are not conducive to one's spiritual growth.

'With Allah is the more excellent abode.' Allah has given us a long rope which we may use either to return to Him or to strangle ourselves. The man of insight (*baṣīrah*, بَصيرَة) does not see grey areas; he sees people either covering up reality (which is the meaning of *kufr*, كُفْور) or being intoxicated by the experience of unity (*tawḥīd*, توحيد). Distinction between these two states becomes clearer as one's insight or inner vision sharpens.

We return to the place where we began: the excellent abode. Through a highly intricate and natural electro-chemical process, we originated from earthly elements. Our bodies were sustained by food from the earth, and to that earth they will return. The other part of our being, our spirit, is meant to be purified, to become aware of duality – of good and bad, health and sickness, poverty and wealth – and to recognize that there is one force from which all creation emanates.

قُلْ أَؤُنَبِّئُكُم بِخَيْرٍ مِّن ذَٰلِكُمْ ۚ لِلَّذِينَ اتَّقَوْا
عِندَ رَبِّهِمْ جَنَّاتٌ تَجْرِي مِن تَحْتِهَا الْأَنْهَارُ
خَالِدِينَ فِيهَا وَأَزْوَاجٌ مُّطَهَّرَةٌ وَرِضْوَانٌ
مِّنَ اللَّهِ ۗ وَاللَّهُ بَصِيرٌ بِالْعِبَادِ

15 **Say: Shall I inform you of what is better than all that? For those who guard fearfully are gardens with their Lord beneath which rivers flow – they abide in them forever – and pure mates, and Allah's pleasure. Allah perceives mankind.**

This verse relates to the previous verse. The love of possessions, the desire to increase one's wealth and the number of one's offspring, all the things that are part of this worldly existence, have been made attractive to man. But the worthiest abode is where there is no change, where there are none of the transient afflictions of this world. Possessions are like treasures put into a boat. The more weight in the hull, the greater the risk of sinking in a stormy sea. A strong and efficient mast and sail – analogous to spiritual strength – are needed to carry it to the destined shore. Possessions are neutralized by spiritual strength.

On the other hand, if the boat has a strong mast but carries little in its hold, it can travel swiftly across the sea, but it will arrive empty. The Muhammadan path is the middle road: 'And thus We have made you a middle nation' (2: 143). It is not a path of outer asceticism or renunciation. The world is to be interacted with; its positive aspects are to be made use of directly, while its negative aspects are out of bounds and to be avoided. The Prophet is the teacher from whom we learn where the boundaries lie, as well as how to avoid transgressing them.

Better than the love of worldly things are the gardens in the presence of the Lord 'For those who guard fearfully'. The word *taqwā* (تقوى) means 'to guard oneself with fear and caution so as to avoid being led astray'. Caution implies prior exposure to a similar situation, thus those who guard fearfully have already been afflicted in the world: they have tried to find solace and comfort in the stuff of this world and have been disappointed. They are cautious about every situation in order to prevent an undesirable outcome, and, because of their sincerity, they are forgiven if they inadvertently participate in an unfortunate situation. Those who continue to take refuge in some aspect of the world – its wealth, its people, its political power – are continually plagued by the nagging fear that one day the security to which they are holding on will no longer be there. Their plastic cards will be redundant because of a massive and universal power shutdown!

'The gardens beneath which rivers flow' are gardens of meaning, condition or state. In this life the experience of physical gardens can give us a taste of a paradisical inner state, a sense of being in a marvellous and fulfilling ambience. The experience, however, does not endure, and people in the midst of the most wonderful and fabulous experiences can be miserable and sad. Something within tells them that the moment of pleasure is not going to last, that they will have to leave. The pleasure is recognized as transient, and thus they cannot totally abandon themselves to it. The heavenly, which is to say permanent, garden is forever fed by subtle and hidden underground rivers. Those invisible waters are preserved forever in the Garden of the next world.

'Pure mates' (*azwāj muṭahhara*, أَزْوَاج مُطَهَّرَة) imply no duality in the Garden; the opposites (*zawj*, زَوْج means a pair) are joined. In this world man seeks woman, the poor seek wealth and the ill seek health. In the next life all seeking is finished. The opposites are continued in pairs; there is no longer any conflict of the two. If a man of faith (*īmān*, إيمان) harboured any unfulfilled desires, those desires would be neutralized to bring about an ultimate equilibrium.

The state of the Garden is described as being like receiving gifts one had not imagined possible. Reality knows the condition of everything, where it is deficient and why. Deficiencies of this world exist in order that we will strive for efficiency, which arises from wisdom and is achieved through the use of the intellect (*'aql*, عقل). One learns how to safeguard one's being and how to be successful. Efficiency clearly indicates the boundaries of action: one is free to act, but only within the limits of general laws which prescribe the paths of action in this world. If one transgresses these bounds, one's freedom is curtailed. If one abuses nature beyond a certain point, the ecology will collapse. The destruction may be so great as to annihilate us in order to effect a return to normal. Allah's will is that we discover that this creation is Allah's, and that we are nothing other than His beloved slaves.

Love of this world can only end in disaster. If the disaster does not occur as several minor or major setbacks or disasters in this life, it will occur as one final calamity at the moment of one's death, because whoever loves this world will not want to leave it. Disappointments in this life caution us against investing in what is transient. The things of this world are a provision, not to be renounced, but to be used and consumed along the journey. For this reason the people of self-knowledge (*'irfān*, عِرْفَان) constantly avoid forming habits. A seeker on the path of self-knowledge may even change the place where he lays his head at night every few days in order not to become complacent in his behaviour. A state of continual change prevents him from becoming too familiar with his surroundings, and so he constantly remembers that his life is transient, that at any given moment he may die. The point of this remembrance is not to produce anxiety or discomfort, but to be grounded in a deeper state of inner peace and tranquillity, irrespective of one's outer struggle or circumstance.

A verse of the Qur'an says, 'O you who believe! Answer Allah and the Messenger when you are called to that which gives you life. Know that Allah intervenes between man and his heart, and that to Him you shall be gathered' (8: 24). Allah is talking to the people of this world, implying that this physical existence is only an example of the real life which is eternal. Each one of us wants to live forever, a desire whose source is divine, but the One who lives forever is the one-and-only Ever-Living (*al-Ḥayy al-Qayyūm*, الحَي القَيُّوم). As created beings we are perishing, but the source of the Ever-living is within us. Once we discover the truth of this, we understand that what we are really adoring and worshipping is the Ever-Living, though this worship of the Eternal is sometimes transformed into actions which are limited to self-preservation. Naturally, it is incumbent upon everyone to preserve their physical well-being as much as possible, for whoever loves the Creator will love what He has given into one's care, yet with the light of intellect one must realize that the body is born to perish. We must therefore strive to live a balanced life, taking care of both our existential and spiritual needs, of both body and soul.

Those who fearfully guard themselves (*muttaqīn*, مُتَّقِين) say that they trust in Allah through reason and natural instinct (*fiṭrah*, فِطْرَة). They understand that there can be no major conflicts in nature that will not be resolved by one force dominating another. For example, we all recognize that we are dying even though we do not want to die. This is a conflict which will not be resolved until we become disillusioned with the nature of our ego-self (*nafs*, نَفْس). When the lower self is surpassed by the higher self through self-knowledge and enlightenment, the conflict is resolved.

The greatest crime one can commit against oneself is to become forgetful of Allah and the truth of His Book. Forgetting Allah comes from forgetting death. When a person says that he has discovered the truth, he is really admitting that the truth was there all the time, but the path he was previously following did not lead to it. He has also discovered that he can never find total fulfilment with any human being. Speaking of humankind, the Qur'an says, 'One of you is an enemy to the other' (2: 36).

Within us are the forces of both evil and good. If one does not act to purify the self, the forces within will produce a Jekyll and Hyde syndrome – with Hyde eventually taking over.

As man grows in faith, his worldly wisdom and sense of discrimination also grow. He becomes more diligent with his use of time and the tools he has been given to work with. His increased sensitivity produces greater effectiveness.

ٱلَّذِينَ يَقُولُونَ رَبَّنَآ إِنَّنَآ ءَامَنَّا فَٱغْفِرْ لَنَا ذُنُوبَنَا
وَقِنَا عَذَابَ ٱلنَّارِ ۝

16 **Those who say: Our Lord, surely we believe, so forgive our faults and save us from the punishment of the Fire.**

The real meaning of forgiveness can be decoded from the Arabic root for forgiveness (*istighfār*, إستغفار) which is *gḥafara* (غفر) meaning 'to cover, protect, correct'. Seeking forgiveness means seeking protection from the results of past errors, and safety from continuing to act erroneously and therefore harmfully. We know the meaning of fire as a physical manifestation without which we cannot survive. Even our nervous system is based on electrical impulses which are a subtle form of fire. Without the fire of the sun, the ecological balance of the earth could not survive. Inner fire is tasted by everyone in the form of anger, anguish, mistrust, greed, hate and jealousy. When time stops, as it eventually will, the experience of this Fire, if it has been fuelled or fed continuously in this life, will then be an ongoing experience in the next level of consciousness. In that zone one will not be able to act, only be acted upon, because the next life is the realm of non-change. Only in this life do we have a measure of freedom to take the initiative.

Freedom is meaningless unless there is constriction. Similarly, a person cannot know the meaning of truth unless he knows what a lie is. While Adam was in the state of the Garden he did not know the duality of truth and falsehood. When the *Shayṭān* made him experience the meaning of a lie, it was through this event that consciousness rose. The fall of Adam was in one sense, therefore, his rise. Had he not fallen, he would have remained in a state of hapless and undiscriminating bliss, similar to that of animals. But once he recognized the trap, he was also shown freedom. As the children of Adam we come into this life in order to gain this recognition experientially. Though we often claim to act for Allah, we know that essentially our obedience to Him is motivated by our own desires: 'If you do good, you do good for your own souls; and if you do evil, it shall be for them' (17: 7).

الصَّابِرِينَ وَالصَّادِقِينَ وَالْقَانِتِينَ وَالْمُنفِقِينَ
وَالْمُسْتَغْفِرِينَ بِالْأَسْحَارِ

17 The patient, the truthful, the humbly obedient, those who spend and those who ask forgiveness before dawn.

Patience (*ṣabr*, صَبْر) is of two types, negative and positive. Being patient with evil whilst one is able to overcome it is to misuse patience. Only when it is impossible to take any action against evil should one wait until the right time or else remove oneself from the situation.

One should be patient with one's aspirations and expectations. Past habits cannot be changed in a few days just as bad posture which has developed over a lifetime cannot be put right in a week. Everything has its own time for healing and reaching fruition. Allah has indicated this by the analogy that He created the heavens and earth in six days (periods). Everything must follow its course, once it has emerged from the uncreated state.

Once one has begun to tread a positive path, patience is very important, because the lower self regularly returns to trick us. *Shaytān* is always present and in order to overcome him we must learn his tricks. Sometimes he comes to us through our emotions, sometimes through reason which encourages us to act wrongly. The secret of being patient is to be impatient with the self, impatient with our faults, our lack of awareness, our heedlessness, greed and laziness. Where we must exercise particular patience is with other people's faults, teaching them with compassion and understanding.

'Those who are truthful' (*ṣādiqīn*, صادِقين) means those who are awakened to their original, naturally noble disposition. Our origin is truth, which each one of us is programmed to seek. When a person knows himself he is steadfast in moments of weakness as well as in moments of strength. With this in mind, one recognizes that gratefulness is especially necessary in moments when life is difficult, when one is most vulnerable and has no outward security. These are in fact the best times. When those times have passed' one looks back upon them as the foundation of one's inner strength. The truth is that we have come from the unknown and we are returning to that unknown; during this journey it is our duty to come to know. If we always keep this in mind, if we admit to our ignorance and face our weaknesses diligently, positively and joyfully, we will overcome them. If instead we hide them, by blowing up the balloon of the ego, death will eventually explode the myth we have created. But if we are constantly able to deflate the ego-self, then death will pose no fear, because, like the transition from sleep to wakefulness, the transition of death will be apparent. The soul simply leaves the body behind and moves into a domain where neither time nor space exists.

Another derivative from the verbal root of the word meaning 'those who are truthful' is 'giving alms' (*ṣadaqah*, صَدَقَة). It is as though by giving charity one is confirming the truth that one owns nothing. When beggars in the East come to any house demanding, 'Give us from the wealth of Allah!', they may sound rude and presumptuous, but what they ask for is their due. Wealth belongs to Allah. Those who are entrusted with it are given the great responsibility of using it properly to help those to whom it has not been given. The beggar in his demand asks how the householder dares to sleep while excess surrounds him and how, when he dies, he will account for it. Alms means giving in order to reflect the truth of Allah's generosity, which is infinite.

'The humbly obedient' (*al-qānitīn*, القانتين) are those who express their servitude to Allah. The act of lifting the hands in supplication (*qunūt*, قُنُوت) is an outer manifestation of obedience to and humility before Allah. If a person inwardly obeys the natural laws, accepts them and works within them, not against them, his inner attitude will be expressed outwardly in gratitude, submission and contentment.

'Those who spend' their wealth and energy on what matters, give what they cherish, not what they no longer want. For example, a parent may take on a dreadful job in order to give his son a good education only to find that after his graduation the boy runs away from home. The son may have done so because the father did not spend of what matters: compassion, understanding, love and attention, rather than money or formal education. We often give what we think is important, not what the situation requires.

'Those who ask forgiveness before dawn. '*Asḥār* (أسحار) is the last part of the night before dawn, when all is quiet and inner focusing is easy. But what is the use of supplicating, praying and meditating at that time if, during the rest of the day, we are in turmoil and confusion? Before dawn all the outer elements are still. The time lends itself to deep and subtle reflection. The Qur'an says, 'Maintain the prayer from the declining of the sun to the darkness of night and the morning recitation; surely the morning recitation is witnessed' (17: 78)

شَهِدَ ٱللَّهُ أَنَّهُۥ لَآ إِلَٰهَ إِلَّا هُوَ وَٱلْمَلَٰٓئِكَةُ وَأُو۟لُوا۟ ٱلْعِلْمِ قَآئِمًۢا بِٱلْقِسْطِ ۚ لَآ إِلَٰهَ إِلَّا هُوَ ٱلْعَزِيزُ ٱلْحَكِيمُ

18 **Allah bears witness that there is no god but He, as do the angels and those who possess knowledge, maintaining justice. There is no god but He, the Mighty, the Wise.**

There is nothing worthy of worship but Him. He is the unique Singular (*Aḥad*, أحَد). He is not just the One (*Wāḥid* وَاحِد), for one implies a second and is the beginning of enumeration. Singularity precedes this, being that Reality from which all manifestation and action have come. Reality witnesses Itself, being Self-sustaining, Self-supporting, Self-knowing and Self-hearing. Allah is the witness to Himself. If we truly want to witness, then we must stop witnessing anything other than Him, for anything other is only a manifestation of Him. The angels witness that there is no god but He because they have no option. They are the powers or forces that participate in holding together the visible parts of this cosmos. Those who have faith and search within themselves come to know with certainty that the existence of anything other than Allah is unacceptable, for it is untrue.

'The angels and those who possess knowledge' establish justice (*qisṭ*, قِسْط). Justice within creation is based on a measure (*qadr*, قَدْر), as the Qur'an states: 'Surely we have created everything according to a measure' (54: 49). Justice implies that laws govern both what is visible and what is invisible. Without these laws there would be chaos.

إِنَّ الدِّينَ عِندَ اللَّهِ الْإِسْلَامُ ۗ وَمَا اخْتَلَفَ الَّذِينَ
أُوتُوا الْكِتَابَ إِلَّا مِن بَعْدِ مَا جَاءَهُمُ الْعِلْمُ بَغْيًا
بَيْنَهُمْ ۗ وَمَن يَكْفُرْ بِآيَاتِ اللَّهِ فَإِنَّ اللَّهَ
سَرِيعُ الْحِسَابِ

19 Surely the life-transaction with Allah is Islam. Those to whom the Book had been given differed only after knowledge had come to them, out of envy among themselves. And whoever disbelieves in the revelations of Allah, then surely Allah is quick in reckoning.

The message and the knowledge that was revealed to all the prophets was the same: it was a map of the path of submission and knowledge of Reality.

'Life-transaction' (*dīn*, دين) is usually translated as 'religion'. The word is related to '*dayn*' (دَيْن) which means 'debt'. The verb means 'to take a loan, borrow, be obligated or humbled'. Thus the correct 'life-transaction' is to honour the debt owed to the Creator. The life-transaction that existed before the Qur'anic revelation was the same.

The people of the revealed books, the Jews, Christians and others, did not differ except in a cultural or historical way. Later many distorted and transgressed the message given to them in the past. Love and attachment to this world led them to interpret the message according to their own fancies. All people are subject to this corruption by taking from the original teaching what is convenient for them to justify their actions or accuse others of wrongdoing. Whatever man does repeatedly becomes attractive and is justified to himself as he is a creature of habit.

This is one of the veils which separates the living from the knowledge of the essence of life.

If we look for faults, we will find faults, and if we look for perfection, we will see perfection. If we use our inner sight we will find perfection in every creation, whereas if we use the outer eye we will find no end to fault in creation. The man of Allah is a man of inner harmony and contentment and of outer struggle and striving at the same time.

No one is independent or separate from this world. The world is what we have made of it, and we cannot escape our respons-ibility for it. In a nuclear disaster we shall all suffer. Whoever exists as a part of a society which has ruined its environment will suffer that ruin along with everyone else. In the meantime, if one has been diligent and has tried to do one's best, at least one is more prepared for and accepting of what is to come.

The person who can look at his actions and intentions and be willing to account for them is indeed fortunate. The willingness to be exposed to one's inner 'balance sheet' helps to bring about spontaneous self-correction. If we are aware of our actions and know why we do them at the moment of their performance, no account is kept; nothing is hidden from moment to moment.

فَإِنْ حَاجُّوكَ فَقُلْ أَسْلَمْتُ وَجْهِيَ لِلَّهِ وَمَنِ اتَّبَعَنِ
وَقُلْ لِلَّذِينَ أُوتُوا الْكِتَابَ وَالْأُمِّيِّينَ
ءَأَسْلَمْتُمْ فَإِنْ أَسْلَمُوا فَقَدِ اهْتَدَوْا وَإِنْ تَوَلَّوْا
فَإِنَّمَا عَلَيْكَ الْبَلَاغُ وَاللَّهُ بَصِيرٌ بِالْعِبَادِ

20 So if they dispute with you, say: I submit myself entirely to Allah and so do those who follow me.

And say to those who have been given the Book and the unlearned people: Do you submit? Then if they submit, they indeed follow the right way, and if they turn away, then your obligation is only to deliver the message. And Allah sees all mankind.

If on some pretext or another a person is faced with an argument or dispute, he could reply by saying that he has submitted to Allah and follows His way. Either one accepts and understands or one does not. Discussing Islam with an egotistic, ignorant person is like discussing different colours with a blind man.

'The unlearned people' refers to the people of Mecca. They had no book or messenger who had risen from among them. On the other hand the majority of the people of Medina were people of the book, the Jews and Christians of that time. The Prophet encouraged people to read and write. 'Ali was the first to record what the Prophet said, and the Companions wrote down and recorded the revelations of the Qur'an.

Allah tells us in this verse that if people embrace Islam they will realize that it is the way to guidance; if they do not, then it is only incumbent upon us to give them the news, to inform in a manner best understood by the listener. It is the Muslim's duty to share the good news; it may be rejected, but that is something over which he has no control. The word used in this verse for 'delivery of the message' (*balāgh*, بَلاَغ) implies deep, profound wisdom. Inherent eloquence (*balāghah*, بَلاَغَة) comes from the same root.

إِنَّ ٱلَّذِينَ يَكْفُرُونَ بِآيَاتِ ٱللَّهِ وَيَقْتُلُونَ
ٱلنَّبِيِّينَ بِغَيْرِ حَقٍّ وَيَقْتُلُونَ ٱلَّذِينَ يَأْمُرُونَ
بِٱلْقِسْطِ مِنَ ٱلنَّاسِ فَبَشِّرْهُم بِعَذَابٍ أَلِيمٍ

21 **Those who disbelieve in the revelations of Allah and slay the prophets unjustly, and slay those among mankind who enjoin justice, announce to them a painful chastisement.**

A prophet's task is to bring the news. He himself has received the revelation and is immersed in a state of knowledge of unity (*tawḥīd*, تَوْحِيد). Those who deny the news because it is incongruous to them either wish to kill the envoy – to destroy what he represents – or seek to destroy his words. If a man has based his entire security on material wealth and is then informed that he has lost it, he would be inclined to disbelieve the news.

There is always a polarization among people around men of knowledge. No prophet ever lived who had the support of the majority of his community early in his lifetime, nor has any master of the path to Allah had an easy time of it. A common saying among people of unity is that no spiritual guide is fully established in his station unless hundreds of good men renounce him. What this means is that there are many degrees of faith and understanding and degrees of truth and submission. The real believer (*mu'min*, مُؤْمِن) trusts that whatever situation he is confronted with has been sent by Allah for him to learn from. With this trust he is able to move on positively without wasting time criticizing and complaining, because he sees nothing other than Allah in all things. If he finds fault with anything, it is with himself: with his wrong judgement, his lack of wisdom, awareness and diligence, and his heedlessness. He blames all of these faults upon himself in order to improve himself.

أُولَٰئِكَ الَّذِينَ حَبِطَتْ أَعْمَالُهُمْ فِي الدُّنْيَا
وَالْآخِرَةِ وَمَا لَهُمْ مِنْ نَاصِرِينَ

22 They are among those whose actions are futile in this world and the Hereafter. They shall have no helpers.

The news reaches them from the outside that they are going to have trouble. Their work and their actions are futile (*ḥabaṭa*, حَبَطَ) and will thus be nullified. If a person does not follow the direction of nature, his or her actions will have no beneficially lasting result. Actions that are not undertaken with the intention of leading one to submission – and to the knowledge that arises from that submission – are worthless. If we envisage one day as a complete cycle of life, at the end of the day we should be content to die, all of our accounts being clear. Such is the state of an awakened being, not of one whose actions are futile.

Once a Bedouin came to 'Alī ibn 'Abī Ṭālib and said, 'I accept everything that you teach, and I accept your logic, but what if there is no Hereafter? 'Alī said: 'If there is no Hereafter, then at least I will have had the best life in the world, for I could not have acted better in this life.' The Bedouin responded, 'That is good enough', and embraced Islam.

أَلَمْ تَرَ إِلَى الَّذِينَ أُوتُوا نَصِيبًا مِنَ الْكِتَابِ
يُدْعَوْنَ إِلَىٰ كِتَابِ اللَّهِ لِيَحْكُمَ بَيْنَهُمْ ثُمَّ يَتَوَلَّىٰ
فَرِيقٌ مِنْهُمْ وَهُمْ مُعْرِضُونَ

23 Have you not seen those who are given a portion of

the Book? They are invited to the Book of Allah that it might decide between them. Then a group of them turn away and they withdraw.

'A portion of the Book' refers to incomplete messages. Before the advent of the Qur'an, man had not reached the stage where he could be given all the divine laws. The Qur'an itself was revealed in stages, and its revelation was not completed until just a few months before the death of the Prophet. When we apply the complete message we must use reasoning, trust and submission, otherwise our inappropriate approach might distort the meaning.

People who have received part of a book or message, or have had some openings of knowledge, are asked to read the whole book to come to the full truth. The reason they do not is because the self finds logical excuses not to. Some believe that their transgressions and wrong-doings will always be forgiven, as happened to the people of Moses. Though they were chastised for a prolonged period of time for their transgressions they still returned to waywardness.

There is a traditional story about two men who entered a mosque. One of them was a scholar, while the other was a known sinner. When they came out of the mosque the sinner was on his way to the Garden but the scholar was on his way to Hell. The reason for this was that the scholar came before Allah arrogantly, with the assumption that he was complete in his piety and knowledge, while the sinner came in shame and humility to pray for redemption, which was granted. The formal worship of the scholar did nothing for him, because it was like any other routine act during the day. The moral is that we cannot always judge a book by its cover; we do not always know what the hidden truth is, what is in the heart. Allah may well be forgiving, but we have no guarantee how, when and to whom forgiveness may be given. Many people commonly ask others to pray for them, but do they pray for themselves? Have they first taken responsibility for their own actions?

ذَٰلِكَ بِأَنَّهُمْ قَالُوا لَن تَمَسَّنَا ٱلنَّارُ إِلَّآ أَيَّامًا مَّعْدُودَٰتٍ
وَغَرَّهُمْ فِى دِينِهِم مَّا كَانُوا يَفْتَرُونَ

24 **This is because they say: The Fire shall not touch us but for a certain number of days; and what they have fabricated deceives them in their life-transaction**

Destruction does not come out of the blue. What happens when we forget the natural and correct way is that we fall into deception (*ghurūr*, غُرور) and false relationships. *Shayṭān* is always there, ready to fill the gap of ignorance and forgetfulness. Laxity, like a vacuum, tends to attract what will fill it, even though the result may be undesirable. It is for this reason a seeker is to avoid idleness at all costs: whatever one does, be it resting, reading, eating, reciting, praying or sleeping, one must do it with conscious awareness. Allah says elsewhere in the Qur'an, 'And when We wish to destroy a town, We send Our commandment to the people who lead luxurious [and frivolous] lives, and transgress therein; thus the word proves true against it; so We destroy it with utter destruction' (17: 16).

فَكَيْفَ إِذَا جَمَعْنَٰهُمْ لِيَوْمٍ لَّا رَيْبَ فِيهِ وَوُفِّيَتْ كُلُّ
كُلُّ نَفْسٍ مَّا كَسَبَتْ وَهُمْ لَا يُظْلَمُونَ

25 **Then how will it be when We shall gather them together on a day about which there is no doubt, and every soul shall be fully repaid for what it has earned. They shall not be dealt with unjustly.**

At the end of time each action will be justly requited – the truth will be exposed. The Qur'an says, 'You shall not be rewarded except for what you did' (36: 54). There is no separation; we are our actions personified. For example, our physical health is the result of our healthy or unhealthy attitudes and actions. We prescribe our future life through our intentions and actions in this life and actions and the final result will be tasted in the Hereafter.

'They shall not be dealt with unjustly': there is injustice in this world, but it is the injustice of man, not Allah's injustice. Allah has created the world in perfect balance and with set boundaries. By keeping to those boundaries we find justice. If we do not keep to them, however, others will appear who will uphold them and will therefore supersede us. In this way cultures and civilizations rise and fall; and people will be shown their hypocrisy when others come who are better than they.

قُلِ ٱللَّهُمَّ مَٰلِكَ ٱلْمُلْكِ تُؤْتِى ٱلْمُلْكَ مَن تَشَآءُ
وَتَنزِعُ ٱلْمُلْكَ مِمَّن تَشَآءُ وَتُعِزُّ مَن تَشَآءُ
وَتُذِلُّ مَن تَشَآءُ بِيَدِكَ ٱلْخَيْرُ إِنَّكَ عَلَىٰ كُلِّ شَىْءٍ قَدِيرٌ

26 **Say: O Allah, Sovereign Master of the Kingdom! You grant the kingdom to whom You please and take the kingdom away from whom You please; You exalt whom You please and abase whom You please; in Your hand is the good. Surely, You have power over all things.**

Allah is the Sovereign Master of all the created kingdoms (*Mālik al-mulk*, مَالِكَ ٱلْمُلْكِ). Appropriate to this verse is the speech given by Zaynab, the sister of Imam Ḥusayn, at the court of *Yazid* in Damascus after the martyrdom of her family. The women who survived the massacre were driven through the desert to his court. There she addressed him: 'Do you imagine, O Yazīd, that because you have taken this vast kingdom and have driven us like slaves, as prisoners of war, that Allah desires evil for us and honour for you? As a result of your victory your arrogance has increased. You have become pleased with yourself and your affairs appear to be smooth. You think now that you have usurped what is our due, and that you are safe. But I am patient. Do you forget what Allah says? "And do not think that to those who are in disbelief we give goodness, we only give them this goodness so that they increase in their criminality, and for them is great pain." '

Imam Ḥusayn's martyrdom in Karbala was a great act of sacrifice, and of defiance of a usurper of 'spiritual leadership' who within his three-year reign had ransacked and destroyed Medina and Mecca.

All goodness and blessings (*khayr*, خَيْر) come from Allah, and Allah's mercy encompasses everyone. Thus, we must expect the best at all times, as our inherent nature (*fiṭrah*, فِطْرَة) expects the best for everybody else. After putting ourselves in other people's shoes, we then become responsible for everything as everything interconnects and relates. The Prophet Moses could not escape all the afflictions which descended upon his people. He was one of them and he shared their suffering.

تُولِجُ ٱلَّيْلَ فِي ٱلنَّهَارِ وَتُولِجُ ٱلنَّهَارَ فِي ٱلَّيْلِ
وَتُخْرِجُ ٱلْحَيَّ مِنَ ٱلْمَيِّتِ وَتُخْرِجُ ٱلْمَيِّتَ مِنَ ٱلْحَيِّ
وَتَرْزُقُ مَن تَشَآءُ بِغَيْرِ حِسَابٍ

27 **You cause the night to pass into the day and the day to pass into the night; You bring forth the living from the dead and You bring forth the dead from the living; and You give sustenance to whom You please without measure.**

The night penetrates into the day and the day penetrates into the night; goodness penetrates into evil and evil into good. The secret and root of everything lies in its opposite. If we want to appreciate good health, we should both remember and avoid illness. If we want to appreciate the wisdom of tranquillity we should catch ourselves at the moment of anger.

The living are brought forth from the dead, and the dead from the living. There is in reality only one source from which everything emanates, but creation appears in pairs and opposites. Man has but one conscience, but two options: right and wrong.

'You have given sustenance to whom You please without measure.' In its general sense, this means sustenance (*rizq*, رزق) from the gross, outer world. But as soon as one has enough food, shelter and clothing, one wants more. The highest sustenance, however, is the knowledge of Allah, and the greatest deprivation is denial, disbelief (*kufr*, كُفْر) and associating anything with Allah (*shirk*, شِرْك). A true seeker has no objective but to be in the pleasure of Allah. The more a man feeds his desires, the greater they grow. He may imagine that satisfaction will come to him through a given event or possession, but he will inevitably find that this assumption is false. Occasionally, if he finds it impossible to control himself, he should give in to the desire. When he has had enough, he must take himself firmly in hand again. Through this experience he will learn his own specific habits, and with that knowledge become better equipped to keep himself in check.

The phrase 'You give sustenance to whom You please without measure' refers to outer and inner gifts, the highest of all being the knowledge of Allah Himself. Those who do not deserve it are those who do not have complete trust. They trust themselves rather than their Creator. This knowledge is a great secret, an open one, which takes great courage to obtain. Allah cannot be touched, smelled, tasted, seen or heard in a physical sense. He will be known in every way once our attention is directed only towards Him. If a man asks how he can be sure of His existence, he is obviously not ready for it. That certainly is the ultimate gift, which requires the ultimate degree of surrender and submission. When man moves one step towards Allah, Allah moves ten steps towards him.

لَا يَتَّخِذِ الْمُؤْمِنُونَ الْكَافِرِينَ أَوْلِيَاءَ مِنْ دُونِ
الْمُؤْمِنِينَ وَمَنْ يَفْعَلْ ذَٰلِكَ فَلَيْسَ مِنَ اللَّهِ فِي شَيْءٍ
إِلَّا أَنْ تَتَّقُوا مِنْهُمْ تُقَاةً وَيُحَذِّرُكُمُ اللَّهُ
نَفْسَهُ وَإِلَى اللَّهِ الْمَصِيرُ

28 **Let not the believers take the non-believers for friends rather than believers; whoever does this shall have nothing from Allah. But you should guard yourselves against them carefully. Allah cautions you about Himself; and to Allah is the final destination.**

Believers (*mu'minūn*, مؤمنون) are different from those without faith, for they have attached themselves to the ever-connecting factor in both this existence and the next. The believer has no will of his own: whatever he does is an aspect of submission and transition into the highest realm of consciousness and inner state. The believer regards this life as a prelude and preparation for the next. He delegates all his needs and fears to his Creator, realizing that any strength he has is derived from his Creator – he is the true slave.

The non-believer (*kāfir*, كافر) denies all this; he is dependent upon himself, and disconnected from Allah's unifying forces. He does not see the one hand of unity behind what appears to be duality and thus suffers from the discordant conflict of opposites. It is impossible for the believer and the non-believer, with such different outlooks and inner states, to be connected in a deeply friendly manner. If they are, then either the believer is not in a state of true faith, or the unbeliever is not really in a state of denial.

'But you should guard yourselves against them.' Allah tells us to have caution by examining and concerning ourselves with the overall circumstances. We have been given an arena in which to act, but we are warned that if we detach ourselves from those who believe, problems will arise. Allah warns us thus: 'Man is a witness upon himself though he may give excuses' (75: 14-15) while Allah is the Witnesser of all that we do. If we find ourselves in a compromising situation, we must extricate ourselves from it urgently. This is particularly true of those who are not strong in spirit. In situations where the only course of action is to dissimulate one's faith, one must know one's strength, for after a short time the weak person will take on the colour of the people with whom he associates.

'And to Allah is the final destination.' Every being returns to Allah together with their intentions and their actions. We must therefore question ourselves at every step, because Allah is questioning us. Each one of us is fully responsible for the extent of our truthfulness or our appeasement with the non-believers. If we spend time with people other than the believers, we should recognize that in some way we have compromised ourselves, and so must ask ourselves how long we are going to continue doing so.

No truly Islamic life can be established unless there is a community, and no community can be established unless the people who constitute it have achieved a certain level of commitment and knowledge. This knowledge cannot come about unless people rally around the best and most knowledgeable among them. Their loyalty can only be as good as the strength of their faith (*īmān*, إيمان), which in turn is dependent upon the state of their hearts. There is no escape from these conditions. If the believers are people who live this life fearlessly and joyfully while preparing for the next, then their actions have direction under the protective umbrella of Islam.

Thus the quality of any community is shaped according to their knowledge and leadership. Every community can potentially be as good as the early community of the Prophet.

It must be remembered that all life is a journey back to the Reality from which we have come. Successful arrival leaves no leeway for straying from the path. This verse is also about subtle hypocrisy (*nifāq*, نِفَاق): we must always ask ourselves why we do the things we do. We are not obliged to judge other people's actions, but we are responsible for our own. Hypocrisy is a very subtle and corrupt vice which needs to be eschewed at all costs. Constant awareness of our inner state is a permanent priority, for death may occur at any time and what we carry with us into the next life is our present inner state.

قُلْ إِن تُخْفُوا مَا فِي صُدُورِكُمْ أَوْ تُبْدُوهُ يَعْلَمْهُ اللَّهُ ۗ
وَيَعْلَمُ مَا فِي السَّمَاوَاتِ وَمَا فِي الْأَرْضِ ۗ
وَاللَّهُ عَلَىٰ كُلِّ شَيْءٍ قَدِيرٌ

29 **Say: Whether you hide what is in your hearts or manifest it, Allah knows it: He knows whatever is in the heavens and the earth. Allah has power over all things.**

Whatever our inner intention may be, it is known to the All-Knowing, whether openly declared or deliberately hidden. The one who is open and exposed to Allah will find no conflicts within himself. One must always examine one's intentions, for however vulgar they may be, once they have been faced one can begin to sublimate them. In confronting one's own vulgarity there is immense benefit, for this act of recognition has in it the reward of unity.

For the ultimate source of all manifestation – subtle or gross – everything is possible. The very 'sourceness' of Allah contains every possible combination of creational systems. Let us imagine that the systems on this earth are like different currents of energy, and that we human beings are propelled from one to another. The millions of these currents may be likened to layers of intermingling energy bands of both a physical and non-physical nature, that hold the cosmos together. Thus, for the man of knowledge there are no miracles: there is only Allah and His manifestations. A miracle is simply an event that occurs without us being able to discern the cause.

All things are possible, but we do not see them as so. Our ignorance and limitation in this regard are a protection and a blessing; otherwise we would not act. If there is anything to be renounced it is nothing other than our own ignorance, our attachments and expectations. The lowest lustful desires can be made to propel man to the highest achievements. It is not the energy of desire that is good or bad in itself: these qualities arise depending on how the energy is used. An electric current may be used both to murder someone or to provide light. Everything is possible for Allah. If a person genuinely asks for forgiveness and turns to Allah, all of his wrong actions will be forgiven.

يَوْمَ تَجِدُ كُلُّ نَفْسٍ مَّا عَمِلَتْ مِنْ خَيْرٍ مُّحْضَرًا ۚ وَمَا عَمِلَتْ
مِن سُوٓءٍ تَوَدُّ لَوْ أَنَّ بَيْنَهَا وَبَيْنَهُۥٓ أَمَدًۢا بَعِيدًا ۗ
وَيُحَذِّرُكُمُ ٱللَّهُ نَفْسَهُۥ ۗ وَٱللَّهُ رَءُوفٌۢ بِٱلْعِبَادِ

30 **On the day when every soul will find present its actions of both good and evil, it shall then wish that between itself and that [evil] there was a great distance. Allah cautions you about Himself; and Allah is kind to mankind.**

This verse is about the universal Day of Reckoning in the next life, the minor resurrection (*al-qiyāmah al-ṣughrā*, القيامة الصغرى) which is the individual's death, and the major resurrection (*al-qiyāmah al-kubrā*, القيامة الكبرى) when all souls are judged. An individual's reckoning can be determined by that person himself – if he is willing to face all aspects of his life and of himself. A great day will come when every self will face and experience the reality of its actions, whether good or evil. When that day arrives, people will actually see how actions are connected with intention, and each person will reap the reward of what he or she has done in accordance with their intentions.

When the Prophet Muhammad travelled from Mecca to the town of Ta'if he was treated very harshly. The abusive inhabitants chased him out of town with stones. In his physical suffering, the Prophet asked Allah not to punish them because they did not understand what they were doing. They mistook the Prophet and his message for their enemy while their own actions were the true enemies. People are enemies of what they do not understand. The man of Allah does not desire punishment for anybody, for he sees only mercy and goodness in this creation.

The experience of life is subject to the temporality of this dimension, while the next consciousness is not. In this verse Allah describes the horror that man will experience when he is confronted with his naked past, unable to clothe it with excuse and hypocrisy. He will wish to distance himself from what he sees. Since the true seeker realizes that he may die at any moment, he will therefore not postpone good actions until tomorrow, for he well knows that tomorrow may never come.

'Allah cautions you about Himself.' We are programmed always to seek harmony and balance in every situation. The balance to be sought is a fine one and often difficult to attain: it is the 'straight path' (*al-ṣirāṭ al-mustaqīm*, الصراط المستقيم). Once a person begins compromising, he is lost. This is what has happened to all religions and ethical or moral codes. Under the illusory banners of education, modernity and progress, people have ended up living in a way that bears no resemblance to the original path. Their hearts are lacking in peace because they have not turned their hearts to Him. This is what Allah cautions us about.

قُلْ إِن كُنتُمْ تُحِبُّونَ ٱللَّهَ فَٱتَّبِعُونِى يُحْبِبْكُمُ ٱللَّهُ وَيَغْفِرْ
لَكُمْ ذُنُوبَكُمْ ۗ وَٱللَّهُ غَفُورٌ رَّحِيمٌ

31 **Say: If you love Allah, then follow me; Allah will love you and forgive your faults, and Allah is Forgiving, Merciful.**

Simply to have seen or heard the Prophet was not enough to transform a person into an enlightened being with total faith and trust in Allah: there was much hypocrisy and mischief, in spite of the Prophet's presence. Ibn ʻAbbas said, 'So many verses were revealed about companions who were hypocrites that we thought none of the companions would be spared.' Their station was dependent upon their inner faith and commitment to Allah and the Messenger.

Allah says that if the believer loves Allah then he wants to know Allah, for knowledge is based on the love of truth. The believer cannot follow the path of Allah in isolation: the complete way is 'the message and the messenger' (*al-risāla wa al-rasūl*, الرِسَالَة والرَسُول). The seeker must follow the messenger and what the messenger represents, which is essentially encoded in the heart. The inner depths of one's heart must be reached so that the Muhammadan echo may resound within. This echo is in turn translated into action, which is known as guided action or something pleasing to Allah. Until and unless the heart dispels its ignorance, fears and attachments, it will not reliably reflect divine inspiration and the higher values. No perfection can be attained except by constantly guarding the mirror of the heart against tarnish.

The man or woman of Allah is constantly in remembrance (*dhikr*, ذِكر), in spontaneous awareness and reflection. Those who are dependent upon Allah are diligent and watchful, and yet confident in their faith and security in Allah's mercy and forgiveness.

قُلْ أَطِيعُوا اللَّهَ وَالرَّسُولَ فَإِن تَوَلَّوْا
فَإِنَّ اللَّهَ لَا يُحِبُّ الْكَافِرِينَ

32 **Say: Obey Allah and the Messenger; but if they turn back, then surely Allah does not love the non-believers.**

The Prophet, the perfect human being, can only show the way: it is up to us to choose to follow and obey. There was no option when we were ejected from the womb, so how can there be confusing options as we move quickly toward the tomb? 'Surely man is unjust, an ingrate!' (14: 34); and 'By the ages, surely, man is in loss' (103: 1-2). He is in loss until, through sufficient suffering, he has come to recognize the true nature of the world. Man must choose submission and obedience because he foolishly ascribes his independence to himself. But Allah is the Lord and man is the slave.

As the child matures, it acquires the ability to discern and the option of obeying or not, just as it has the choice to recognize what is right and what is wrong. The Prophet was only a messenger: 'You are not a watcher over them' (88: 22). The Prophet is not responsible for people's actions: 'Nothing is incumbent upon the Messenger but to deliver the message' (5: 99). Whatever might befall people was not in his hands; but because of the love that prophets had for their people, they often appeared to be greatly concerned and almost in pain for others – as the Qur'an says: 'Perhaps you will kill yourself with grief because they do not believe' (26: 3).

Most people live as if in a state of sleep from which they cannot be awakened. The only thing that can stop man from abusing himself and others is that inner knowledge in his heart which brings peace and harmony. For the man of faith it is necessary only for him to repeat that he has been given a most beautiful situation, the most perfect creation of the absolutely perfect Creator.

'But if they turn back.' By turning away from obedience to Allah and His Messenger they have in fact denied themselves. They have cut off their very roots. This is not the Prophet's curse upon them, it is the law of Reality. Whoever goes against it will inevitably meet his doom.

إِنَّ ٱللَّهَ ٱصْطَفَىٰٓ ءَادَمَ وَنُوحًا وَءَالَ إِبْرَٰهِيمَ
وَءَالَ عِمْرَٰنَ عَلَى ٱلْعَٰلَمِينَ

33 Surely Allah chose Adam and Noah and the descendants of Abraham and the descendants of Imran above the nations.

Creation follows a hierarchical order; there is no uniformity. There is, however, equity and justice. Adam was selected from all other creatures, just as the Prophet Noah was selected from among his people. Noah recognized the coming flood to be a reaction against his people for their wrongful deeds. His situation was like that of the educated agronomist who, when visiting a village in India, discovered a supply of deadly chemicals on a farm. The farmer had been given these chemicals to clear his land of weeds in order to plant a new crop. The agronomist knew that these chemicals were so fatal that the whole family would be at risk, so he tried to save them, to no avail. Finally he left, having failed to convince the farmer, but saving his own life from the deadly poison. In the same way, the Prophet Noah knew that his people's ignorant actions were going to bring about destruction, and he warned them. His final act was to save himself and whatever else he could in the safety of the Ark.

The Qur'an states that Allah can erase all man's wrongdoing so that he may start afresh. However, tremendous effort is needed for this 'new life' to occur. It cannot be obtained simply by making a supplication with a list of desired requests; one must strive for it. The angel Gabriel said to Mary, 'And shake the trunk of the palm tree towards you; it will drop fresh ripe dates upon you' (19: 25). The blessings are there, but we must shake the tree. For the person of inner purity and perception, a little effort generates a greater result, because this person is precise and inspired in knowledge and action. The one with less developed awareness and ability must strive much harder before he succeeds. The man or woman of pure heart sees what others do not see, because the eyes of those others are veiled by their own desires and attachments.

ذُرِّيَّةً بَعْضُهَا مِن بَعْضٍ ۗ وَاللَّهُ سَمِيعٌ عَلِيمٌ

34 **Offspring, one from the other; and Allah is Hearing, Knowing.**

First Allah created the human being to be His representative on earth, and selected Adam from whom all humankind is descended. In this way Allah has selected each one of us. After Adam came Noah, who was the first of the five great messengers, the others being Abraham, Moses, Jesus and Muhammad. They were resolute (*ūlū al-'azm*, أُولُو الْعَزْم) in fulfilling their role of bringing the message, and because of their resolution they were given wisdom, the book, and the Divine Law. Moses and Jesus were from the descendants of 'Imrān, both genetically and spiritually.

All the prophets were 'chosen' (*musṭaṭūn*, مُصْطَفُون), which comes from a verbal root meaning 'to be pure' (*ṣafā*, صَفَا). They were perfect beings. There is a clear and familial connection between them. Transmission of wisdom and knowledge, however, does not take place only through heredity. Noah's son rejected him and perished. There are many other examples where the close relatives rejected the truth. Heredity, though an important factor, is not the only one: it can also be detrimental. 'He brings forth the living from the dead' (6: 95): a child's parents may be as spiritually dead as the child is spiritually alive. They may be living in darkness and denial of Allah, yet the child may be an awakened believer.

إِذْ قَالَتِ امْرَأَتُ عِمْرَانَ رَبِّ إِنِّي نَذَرْتُ لَكَ مَا فِي بَطْنِي
مُحَرَّرًا فَتَقَبَّلْ مِنِّي ۖ إِنَّكَ أَنتَ السَّمِيعُ الْعَلِيمُ

35 **When 'Imran's wife said: My Lord, surely I vow to You what is in my womb, freely, [to be devoted] to Your service; accept therefore from me. Surely, You are the Hearing, the Knowing.**

فَلَمَّا وَضَعَتْهَا قَالَتْ رَبِّ إِنِّي وَضَعْتُهَا أُنثَىٰ وَاللَّهُ أَعْلَمُ بِمَا
وَضَعَتْ وَلَيْسَ الذَّكَرُ كَالْأُنثَىٰ ۖ وَإِنِّي سَمَّيْتُهَا مَرْيَمَ وَإِنِّي أُعِيذُهَا بِكَ
وَذُرِّيَّتَهَا مِنَ الشَّيْطَانِ الرَّجِيمِ

36 **So when she delivered, she said: My Lord, I have brought forth a female. Allah knew best what she brought forth; the male is not like the female. I have named her Mary [Maryam in Arabic], and I seek refuge in You, for her and her offspring from the accursed Shayṭān.**

Allah has woven all the offspring of the Prophet Adam together through the natural fabric of creation. He now presents the example of a pure heart, one which is completely in that eternal, joyful state of communion with Allah. The wife of 'Imrān, the mother of Mary, vows that the unborn child in her womb will be dedicated to serve the cause of Allah, and will be free of any personal demands and expectations. From us comes the intention, but from Allah comes the ultimate result. The wife of Imran was inspired to pledge her child to serve in the temple or place of worship, and here she asks that her offer be accepted.

This is not a dialogue which took place in time: rather it describes the inner dimension of people immersed in divine knowledge. When the mother of Mary realized that she had given birth to a girl, she said, 'This is a girl, but of course, Allah already knew what was in my womb.' Following this she said, 'The male is not the same as the female.' This could be interpreted as a sign of disappointment, because a female was not of the same status as a male in the temple rituals (for example, a woman cannot enter the house of worship while menstruating), but in fact it illustrates the depth of commitment Mary's mother had to Allah. Mary's mother asks Allah to protect her offspring from *Shayṭān*, for the higher the knowledge and spiritual station of a person, the greater the polarization between the good and evil around him.

Mary's mother had obviously realized that her vow was to be of major significance in the unfolding of creation. The Mosaic doctrine had been distorted for hundreds of years by the Rabbis; and we can understand how a pure woman could recognize in her heart that the message was no longer being transmitted correctly, that it was not being related as it had come from the Prophet Moses. Her prayers were, in fact, for a revival. She wanted to bring forth a being who would purify the path to Allah. We know that she was the wife of a great man and that she herself was of a high spiritual rank; she too was one of the 'chosen'.

How then could she have been disappointed, when she was already appointed by Allah to Allah? Whoever has trust in Allah must also have certainty that whatever takes place is for the ultimate good. Allah's ways are most subtle, and are not always instantaneously understood by us in our limited knowledge.

The Qur'an is not an ordinary book. If it were, then it would be merely a disjointed historical record. This verse describes the purity of a vow or solemn pledge (*nadhr*, نَذْر). Once one has made a vow, one must trust in Allah. Being a woman of high station, the mother of Mary must have realized that something extraordinary was going to happen. She named her daughter Mary, which in the language of those days meant 'the slave, the one in prostration, the servant'.

Allah's plan in fact was far more extraordinary than Mary's mother could have imagined. His aim was to create a man without a father, because the people of the time had become so decadent that a powerful miracle was needed to make an impact upon them. This condition of social degeneracy remained unchanged until the time of Muhammad, when the miracle became the man himself, the perfected, universal man.

فَتَقَبَّلَهَا رَبُّهَا بِقَبُولٍ حَسَنٍ وَأَنْبَتَهَا نَبَاتًا
حَسَنًا وَكَفَّلَهَا زَكَرِيَّا كُلَّمَا دَخَلَ عَلَيْهَا زَكَرِيَّا الْمِحْرَابَ
وَجَدَ عِنْدَهَا رِزْقًا قَالَ يَا مَرْيَمُ أَنَّىٰ لَكِ هَٰذَا قَالَتْ هُوَ مِنْ عِنْدِ اللَّهِ
إِنَّ اللَّهَ يَرْزُقُ مَنْ يَشَاءُ بِغَيْرِ حِسَابٍ

37 **So her Lord accepted her graciously, and made her grow up well, and assigned her to the charge of Zachariah. Whenever Zachariah entered the sanctuary, he found her with sustenance. He said: O Mary, from where does this come to you? She said: It is from Allah; surely, Allah gives to whom He pleases without measure.**

Allah accepted her supplications, and her destiny was as she desired. There was a dispute as to who would look after Mary, because her father 'Imrān had died. Lots were drawn, and the Prophet Zachariah took charge of her upbringing.

The word for 'sustenance' (*rizq*, رزْق) means provision, both materially and otherwise. Knowledge is a high form of sustenance; purification of the heart is spiritual sustenance of an even higher degree. What is the use of food and air, unless it is going to increase man's faith and knowledge? We are dependent in every way upon Allah, both outwardly and inwardly. We show courtesy to the creation of Allah, and yet our submission and real courtesy is toward the Creator.

The word translated here as 'sanctuary' (*miḥrāb*, مِحْراب) also means the niche in the sanctuary that indicates the direction of prayer. Its root (*ḥāraba*, حارَب) means 'to make war'. Thus, the prayer-niche is also referred to allegorically as the place of war, because it is where one does battle with the lower self. Mary probably spent much of her time in the place of prayer, as this was a priority in her life.

Whenever Zachariah came to her, presumably to ask after her health and needs, he found her well, contentedly immersed in prayer; and the physical means of sustenance were available to her. When asked how this was, she replied, 'Surely, Allah gives to whom he pleases without measure.' But how do we reconcile this statement? For as Allah also says, 'He created everything, then ordained for it a measure' (25: 2). Surely Allah's decrees and measures differ from the bases of man's reasoning and calculation. Also, when there is purity in the heart, another type of energy becomes available. It is related that Ali's diet often consisted of bread and onion with no third item. His physical strength, stamina, courage and endurance are difficult to explain given the meagreness and simplicity of his daily diet.

هُنَالِكَ دَعَا زَكَرِيَّا رَبَّهُ ۖ قَالَ رَبِّ هَبْ لِي مِن لَّدُنكَ
ذُرِّيَّةً طَيِّبَةً ۖ إِنَّكَ سَمِيعُ الدُّعَاءِ

38 **There did Zachariah supplicate to his Lord saying: My Lord grant me from Your presence goodly offspring; surely, You are the One who hears supplication.**

When Zachariah witnessed Allah's immense mercy and compassion, his heart opened and he saw the possibility of the impossible through Allah. At that moment his heart called upon his Lord to grant him 'a goodly offspring!'

فَنَادَتْهُ الْمَلَائِكَةُ وَهُوَ قَائِمٌ يُصَلِّي فِي الْمِحْرَابِ
أَنَّ اللَّهَ يُبَشِّرُكَ بِيَحْيَىٰ مُصَدِّقًا بِكَلِمَةٍ مِنَ اللَّهِ
وَسَيِّدًا وَحَصُورًا وَنَبِيًّا مِنَ الصَّالِحِينَ

39 **Then the angels called to him as he stood praying in the sanctuary: Allah gives you the good news of John [Yahya in Arabic], a verifier of the word from Allah, honourable and chaste, a prophet from among the righteous ones.**

The Prophet Zachariah was informed of what was to come: he would have a son called John who would confirm (*muṣaddiq*, مُصدِّق) the divine message of Allah through Jesus (*'Isa* in Arabic). In other words, John would be a prophet in his own right, and a companion and sanctioner of the great Prophet Jesus.

قَالَ رَبِّ أَنَّىٰ يَكُونُ لِي غُلَامٌ وَقَدْ بَلَغَنِيَ الْكِبَرُ
وَامْرَأَتِي عَاقِرٌ قَالَ كَذَٰلِكَ اللَّهُ يَفْعَلُ مَا يَشَاءُ

40 **He said: My Lord, how shall I have a son when old age has already come upon me, and my wife is barren. He said: Even thus does Allah what He pleases.**

After the moment of his heart's inspiration (*waḥy*, وَحي), Zachariah's humanity raised its voice, asking how this might be. He was speaking with the voice of reason and limitation, for he was an old man, according to narrated tradition perhaps a hundred or more years of age, while his wife was in her late nineties and barren.

'Even thus does Allah what He pleases': Allah's power has no limit. For each of His rules there is an exception; otherwise, there could not be a rule. Man must consider all the normal and natural factors in a situation, not the abnormal, miraculous or exceptional.

قَالَ رَبِّ اجْعَل لِّي آيَةً ۖ قَالَ آيَتُكَ أَلَّا تُكَلِّمَ
النَّاسَ ثَلَاثَةَ أَيَّامٍ إِلَّا رَمْزًا ۗ وَاذْكُر رَّبَّكَ كَثِيرًا
وَسَبِّحْ بِالْعَشِيِّ وَالْإِبْكَارِ

41 **He said: My Lord, appoint a sign for me. Said He: your sign is that you shall not speak to men for three days except by signs; remember your Lord much, and glorify [Him] in the evening and in the morning.**

Zachariah asked for an outward sign to confirm the angelic inspiration and Allah answered him; he would not be able to speak to anyone for three days except by signs (*ramz*, رَمْز). When that occurred, he would know that his wife was pregnant. The inner meaning of this verse is that outer confirmation comes when the time is right.

The three days were days of restraint from speech. Restraint of the senses increases the seeker's sensitivity to the unseen, and enhances the state of remembrance and awareness. Man naturally aspires to see the perfection behind everything that happens; he yearns to know the cause behind every effect. That state of knowledge is accessible only through a trusting and purified heart.

وَإِذْ قَالَتِ الْمَلَائِكَةُ يَا مَرْيَمُ إِنَّ اللَّهَ اصْطَفَاكِ وَطَهَّرَكِ وَاصْطَفَاكِ عَلَىٰ نِسَاءِ الْعَالَمِينَ

42 And when the angels said: O Mary, surely Allah has chosen you and purified you, choosing you above all the women of the world.

This and the next verse continue the story of Mary. She was inspired, and assured that she was among the select ones. The word 'chosen' (*muṣṭafā*, مُصْطَفَى) is a name by which the Prophet Muhammad is also referred to. She had been chosen 'above all the women of the world' because she had, from the very beginning of her life, aspired to be that which her mother had desired for her. It is related that she had no menstrual cycle, and as a confirmation of her unique position among women, she became pregnant without ever having been touched by a man, giving birth to the Prophet Jesus. She was so utterly devoted to Allah that she depended on no one but Him.

يَا مَرْيَمُ اقْنُتِي لِرَبِّكِ وَاسْجُدِي وَارْكَعِي مَعَ الرَّاكِعِينَ

43 O Mary, be obedient to your Lord, prostrate and bow down with those who bow.

Obedience, prostration and bowing are devotional elements in which one dissolves inwardly into the One Whom one worships. Allah tells Mary to be amongst other people 'who bow'. He tells her to share the light of her devotion and prayers with others. Sometimes it is best to act anonymously or remain in isolation, while at other times it is best to act publicly or be among people. This verse clearly indicates that both men and women benefit from worshipping with others.

ذَٰلِكَ مِنْ أَنۢبَآءِ ٱلْغَيْبِ نُوحِيهِ إِلَيْكَ ۚ وَمَا كُنتَ لَدَيْهِمْ
إِذْ يُلْقُونَ أَقْلَٰمَهُمْ أَيُّهُمْ يَكْفُلُ مَرْيَمَ
وَمَا كُنتَ لَدَيْهِمْ إِذْ يَخْتَصِمُونَ

44 **This is information from the Unseen which We reveal to you. You were not with them when they cast lots [to decide] which of them would have charge of Mary, and you were not with them when they contended with one another.**

This verse refers to verse 37, recounting the time when Zachariah was appointed as Mary's guardian. Arrows had been used to draw lots, and it was by this method of selection that Zachariah became her guardian.

'You were not with them when they cast their lots.' This knowledge came from the Unseen (*Ghayb*, غَيْب), from Allah. It is implied that at the time of the Prophet Muhammad nobody was sure how these events had occurred.

The men who wanted to look after Mary were competing with one another for the honour. There are other descriptions of competition in the Qur'an, such as, 'Hasten to forgiveness from your Lord and to a garden the expanse of which is as the expanse of the heavens and the earth' (57: 21). Positive competition for the opportunity to perform goodness is considered an act of worship.

إِذْ قَالَتِ ٱلْمَلَٰٓئِكَةُ يَٰمَرْيَمُ إِنَّ ٱللَّهَ يُبَشِّرُكِ بِكَلِمَةٍ مِّنْهُ
ٱسْمُهُ ٱلْمَسِيحُ عِيسَى ٱبْنُ مَرْيَمَ وَجِيهًا فِى ٱلدُّنْيَا
وَٱلْءَاخِرَةِ وَمِنَ ٱلْمُقَرَّبِينَ

45 **When the angels said: O Mary, surely Allah gives you good news of a word from Him. His name is the Messiah, Jesus, the son of Mary, worthy of regard in this world and the Hereafter, and he will be among those who are close [to Allah].**

In verse 39 of this chapter, the Prophet Jesus is referred to as 'a word from Allah' and also as 'the Messiah' (*masīḥ*, مَسيح), that is, 'the anointed one'. The root of the word for messiah means 'to wipe clean' (*masaḥa*, مَسَحَ). This name indicates complete purification from sin or error. Whatever Jesus touched with his hand was rendered healed and whole.

وَيُكَلِّمُ ٱلنَّاسَ فِى ٱلْمَهْدِ وَكَهْلًا وَمِنَ ٱلصَّٰلِحِينَ

46 **And he shall speak to the people when he is in the cradle and when he is of mature age, and he shall be among the righteous ones.**

Not only was this being born of extraordinary circumstances, but he himself was an extraordinary, perfect being. Mary was assured that her son was to be a prophet of great wisdom and unusual divine qualities.

قَالَتْ رَبِّ أَنَّىٰ يَكُونُ لِي وَلَدٌ وَلَمْ يَمْسَسْنِي بَشَرٌ

قَالَ كَذَٰلِكِ اللَّهُ يَخْلُقُ مَا يَشَاءُ ۚ إِذَا قَضَىٰ أَمْرًا

أَمْرًا فَإِنَّمَا يَقُولُ لَهُ كُن فَيَكُونُ

47 **She said: My Lord, how shall I bear a son and no man has touched me? He said: Even so, Allah creates what He pleases; when He has decreed a matter, He only says to it: Be, and it is!**

We always reason and look for cause and effect in events and experiences. In her wonderment over what had happened to her, Mary asked how it could be, since no man had ever even touched her. The angel Gabriel may have answered her, but we cannot comprehend the nature of such communication. In any case, Mary received her knowledge in a voice which said, 'Allah creates what He pleases.' She was in a state of wonderment because of the lack of physical conception. Then she was told that it was indeed possible to conceive a child by the sheer will of Reality. Cause and effect constitute a norm, a general trend of laws, yet for every norm there is a situation which is not normal to man's understanding – but is still within the norm of Reality.

وَيُعَلِّمُهُ الْكِتَابَ وَالْحِكْمَةَ وَالتَّوْرَاةَ وَالْإِنجِيلَ

48 **And He will teach him the Book, the Wisdom, the Torah and the Gospel.**

The divine books that had been revealed were made known to Jesus. Mary was told that he would know the Book of Reality, that he would know what is written as well as its Author. He would have wisdom, and knowledge of the Old Testament and the Gospels. These books were for the people of his time, part of the one and only eternal Book of Allah.

وَرَسُولًا إِلَىٰ بَنِي إِسْرَائِيلَ أَنِّي قَدْ جِئْتُكُمْ بِآيَةٍ مِنْ
رَبِّكُمْ ۖ أَنِّي أَخْلُقُ لَكُمْ مِنَ الطِّينِ كَهَيْئَةِ الطَّيْرِ فَأَنْفُخُ فِيهِ
فَيَكُونُ طَيْرًا بِإِذْنِ اللَّهِ ۖ وَأُبْرِئُ الْأَكْمَهَ وَالْأَبْرَصَ
وَأُحْيِي الْمَوْتَىٰ بِإِذْنِ اللَّهِ ۖ وَأُنَبِّئُكُمْ بِمَا تَأْكُلُونَ
وَمَا تَدَّخِرُونَ فِي بُيُوتِكُمْ ۚ إِنَّ فِي ذَٰلِكَ لَآيَةً لَكُمْ
إِنْ كُنْتُمْ مُؤْمِنِينَ

49 **He will be a messenger to the Children of Israel [saying]: I have come to you with a sign from your Lord. I make for you out of clay the form of a bird, then I breathe into it and it becomes a bird by the permission of Allah. I heal the blind and the leprous, and I bring the dead to life with Allah's permission. I inform you of what you should eat and what you should store in your houses. Most surely there is a sign in this for you if you are believers.**

Mary continued to be informed, through revelation, of what was to happen to her son. He would be a messenger to the Children of Israel (*Banī Isrā'il*). He would have signs and powers given to him by his Lord, proving to men that he was no ordinary being, and that his message was no ordinary information or news. He would be able to bring life to inanimate matter, such as a clay bird, by the permission of Allah. He would be a conduit, an instrument of divine power, not divinity itself. He would be able to perform other miracles such as healing the blind (*akmah*, أكمة) and the lepers (*abraṣ*, أبرص). He would also bring the dead to life. All this would be done by the permission (*idhn*, إذن) of Allah. The verbal root of the word permission means 'to hear', implying that an act can be done when the order to do it has been heard; man, therefore, is simply a conduit.

The Prophet Jesus himself said that everything came from Allah, and that he could do his work only by the grace of Allah. The will of Jesus and Allah's decree were unified. This illustrates an important aspect of unity. Jesus did not desire to force upon his people the divine message that he brought; no man, not even a prophet, is given that responsibility. The Qur'an says, 'You cannot guide whom you love' (25: 56), and yet elsewhere it says, 'Most surely you show the way to the right path' (12: 52). What is indicated is that the notion of self must be abandoned: the self is stripped away, leaving only the decrees of Allah; then transformation can take place for those who trust and follow the Messenger of Allah.

Jesus was given, by the permission of Allah, much more than an inexplicable power that could bring life to the dead or sight to the blind. The Qur'an repeatedly informs us that the miracles he performed were for those who trusted that everything emanates from one Reality. These signs helped to confirm that faith for them. For those who had no faith, the miracles were seen as magic, or as a series of mere coincidences.

Jesus' miracles were the bond that attached people to his message. In his time, people believed more readily in the divine origin of these occurrences, whereas nowadays many of his miracles could perhaps be interpreted more scientifically. Apparent miraculousness is the interaction of multiple factors at play in the zone of time and space, not all of which are accessible to our understanding. Therefore, like the scientist who understands the processes that are taking place in front of him, the prophet sees nothing strange in what takes place around him or as a result of his own actions. The only thing that remains strange for the man of knowledge, and especially for a prophet, is that people continue to wonder over the process of their own unfolding. Men of knowledge are baffled by the lack of urgency in others for the attainment of higher knowledge and awakening.

The verse says that Jesus could inform people about what they were hiding in their houses. The Prophet Muhammad said: 'Beware of the believer's insight.' One who sees through the eye of unity sees far more than just what the physical eye perceives. What appears to us as odd or miraculous is due to the grossness of our outer perception.

وَمُصَدِّقًا لِّمَا بَيْنَ يَدَيَّ مِنَ التَّوْرَىٰةِ وَلِأُحِلَّ لَكُم
بَعْضَ الَّذِي حُرِّمَ عَلَيْكُمْ وَجِئْتُكُم بِـَٔايَةٍ مِّن رَّبِّكُمْ
فَاتَّقُوا اللَّهَ وَأَطِيعُونِ

50 **And [I come as] a verifier of the Torah which is in my hands in order that I may allow you part of what has been forbidden to you. I have come to you with a sign from your Lord, so guard carefully for Allah, and obey me.**

Jesus confirmed what his people originally believed in, that is, the Torah, and he came to revive its spirit and clarify some aspects of its teachings. Some of the rules of the Law were being misused or had been discarded. For example, a story appears in the Gospels concerning the stoning of an adulteress. Stoning to death as a punishment for adultery was ordained in the Torah, but the law was being abused among the Jews. Jesus declares that no one could stone an adulteress unless they themselves were free of sin: 'Which one of you is without sin?' he asks as a group of men was about to stone a woman; their reply was to walk away. The account of the incident ends at this point. In the Qur'an, however, it is quite clear that there must be four just men (*'udūl*, عُدوُل) who witnessed the act in order for the woman to be declared an adulteress. The men must be reputably trustworthy, and known for their good conduct.

Jesus brought not only a revival, but an improvement of what had existed before: with the passage of time since Moses, the nature of the social change that had been wrought necessitated this. Reality is unchanging, but the Law required an improved expression: for example, at the time of Moses, man had evolved from a hunter-gatherer to more of a city dweller. A polarity existed between the rigid, Pharaonic, centralized system and the nomadic culture, and the Mosaic law reflected this socio-cultural change.

Each message as brought by its messenger reflected man's thrust forward into time. The Prophet Muhammad was the final link in the chain. The Islam of Muhammad had its own evolutionary cycle, developing over a period of twenty-three years and resulting in a code of Law (*Sharī'ah*, شريعة) applicable to every human situation, valid for the rest of man's existence on earth.

إِنَّ ٱللَّهَ رَبِّى وَرَبُّكُمْ فَٱعْبُدُوهُ هَٰذَا صِرَٰطٌ مُّسْتَقِيمٌ

51 Surely, Allah is my Lord and your Lord, therefore serve Him; this is the straight path.

The Prophet Jesus declares that he is not a god and that he is not to be worshipped, for his life emanates from the One whom he worships. He commands men to serve their Lord and uphold that covenant (as on a straight path), and thereby fulfil the purpose of creation.

فَلَمَّآ أَحَسَّ عِيسَىٰ مِنْهُمُ ٱلْكُفْرَ قَالَ مَنْ أَنصَارِىٓ إِلَى ٱللَّهِ
قَالَ ٱلْحَوَارِيُّونَ نَحْنُ أَنصَارُ ٱللَّهِ ءَامَنَّا بِٱللَّهِ
وَٱشْهَدْ بِأَنَّا مُسْلِمُونَ

52 **But when Jesus perceived unbelief on their part, he said: Who are my helpers in Allah's way? The disciples said: We are Allah's helpers. We believe in Allah, so bear witness that we are ones who have submitted.**

Like all prophets before him, Jesus encountered major resistance from the people of his culture because of the vested interests of existing power groups, habits, fears and ignorance. When he sensed that they would continue in their denial of his message, he separated the believers from the hypocrites, the believers being known as the 'helpers' (*anṣār*, أَنْصَار).

The word translated as 'disciples' (*ḥawārīyyūn*, حَوَاريون) has several interesting shades of meaning, for example 'to return, recede, decrease, diminish'. Thus they diminished their egos and returned to their Source. Another facet of meaning is 'to change, alter, amend, transform': for they were transformed by the message of Jesus. Yet another meaning is 'to bleach', which signifies purification.

'Alī was once asked what the phrase 'ones who have submitted' meant in the last part of the verse. He said that true submission (*taslīm*, تَسليم) leads to certainty (*yaqīn*, يَقين) which in turn leads to confirmation (*taṣdīq*, تَصْديق). Put another way, those who have certainty about Allah confirm it by their intentions and deeds. Confirmation firmly establishes this certainty and leads to realization (*adā'*, أداء). The realized being takes his total life transaction (*dīn*, دين) directly from his Lord.

A person's faith can be judged by his actions. The non-believer (*kāfir*, كافر) is known by the degree of his confusion, ignorance and denial. The life-transaction of the non-believer is in direct opposition to the way of submission, Islam. They do not mix. Islam is the original life-transaction (*dīn al-fiṭrah*, دين الفطرة) upon which man's nature is created and formed. Even wrongs within the bounds of Islam are better than the good deeds performed beyond its limits. It is said that the mistakes of those close to Allah (singular *walī*, ولي) are better than the virtues of those who are not. Anything done with good intentions and in submission, but which results in a wrong outcome, is forgiven, but good deeds done for any reason other than coming close to Allah will ultimately be of no lasting benefit.

Thus, the men who were around the Prophet Jesus said, 'We are in submission. We accept the truth and will abide by it. We will come to his aid because we are part of his message. Our lives are transformed, for now we know.'

رَبَّنَا آمَنَّا بِمَا أَنزَلْتَ وَاتَّبَعْنَا الرَّسُولَ فَاكْتُبْنَا مَعَ الشَّاهِدِينَ

53 **Our Lord, we believe in what You have revealed and we follow the messenger, so write us down among those who bear witness.**

Jesus' close followers declared what was within them. They announced their trust in the message he brought and their commitment and intention to follow him.

وَمَكَرُوا وَمَكَرَ اللَّهُ وَاللَّهُ خَيْرُ الْمَاكِرِينَ

54 **They planned and Allah planned, and Allah is the best of planners.**

The enemies of Jesus plotted to kill him, to eradicate what they perceived as a threat to their system. The verbal root of the word for 'planned' (*makara*, مَكَرَ) also means 'to cheat, plot, double-cross'.

Man's plan for his life will come to nought unless it is in accordance with the divine decree. A time comes when man's ignorance and misadventure will work against him. Allah's laws will always naturally and spontaneously overcome human plans which do not lead in the direction of His creational decree. Man is given freedom within a limited scope; when he reaches the boundaries of that freedom, another set of factors comes into play. Allah's ultimate plan is to cause us to recognize Him. We are given limits so that we may be brought to submission, to make us understand that there is no way out of the created order. Allah's plan is permanently operative at all levels of creation. The ink is dry on His decree, but it is still described to us in dynamic terms in order for us to recognize that ultimate freedom lies in freeing ourselves from the chains of the ego-self. Wherever we turn we will come to see this. 'Where is there to flee?' (75: 10).

إِذْ قَالَ ٱللَّهُ يَٰعِيسَىٰٓ إِنِّى مُتَوَفِّيكَ وَرَافِعُكَ إِلَىَّ وَمُطَهِّرُكَ
مِنَ ٱلَّذِينَ كَفَرُوا۟ وَجَاعِلُ ٱلَّذِينَ ٱتَّبَعُوكَ فَوْقَ ٱلَّذِينَ
كَفَرُوٓا۟ إِلَىٰ يَوْمِ ٱلْقِيَٰمَةِ ثُمَّ إِلَىَّ مَرْجِعُكُمْ فَأَحْكُمُ
فَأَحْكُمُ بَيْنَكُمْ فِيمَا كُنتُمْ
فِيهِ تَخْتَلِفُونَ

55 **And when Allah said: O Jesus, I shall cause you to die, raise you to Me, and purify you of those who disbelieve. I shall place those who follow you above those who disbelieve until the Day of Reckoning. Then all of you will return to Me, and I shall make the judgement about your differences.**

There are two words for 'death' in Arabic, both of which appear in the Qur'an. One implies physical death (*mawt*, مَوْت), while the word used in this verse implies faithfulness and loyalty (*wafah*, وَفَاة) in having fulfilled an obligation. Here Allah says that He will take Jesus to Himself, that Jesus has been saved and returned to Him. Elsewhere the Qur'an tells us clearly that Jesus did not die a normal death, nor was he crucified:

'And their saying: Surely, we have killed the Messiah, Jesus, son of Mary, the messenger of Allah. They did not kill him nor did they crucify him, but it appeared to them that this was the case. Most surely those who differ therein only express an opinion based on inconsistencies. They have no real knowledge in regard to this opinion, but follow only conjectures. Surely, they did not kill him. Rather, Allah raised him up to Himself; and Allah is Mighty, Wise' (4: 157-158).

Allah says that He raised Jesus up to His presence, purified him and gave him comfort from those who disbelieved, and that those who followed him would be above those who denied until the Day of Reckoning. Whoever believes in that message, whoever believes in unity (*tawḥīd*, توحيد) while in this world, will also be raised up to a higher station.

فَأَمَّا ٱلَّذِينَ كَفَرُوا۟ فَأُعَذِّبُهُمْ عَذَابًا شَدِيدًا
فِى ٱلدُّنْيَا وَٱلْءَاخِرَةِ وَمَا لَهُم مِّن نَّـٰصِرِينَ

56 Then as for those who disbelieve, I will punish them severely in this world and in the Hereafter, and they shall have no helpers.

Those who deny the message in this world already taste the discomfort and agitation of fear, insecurity and the purposelessness of life, all as a prelude to the next life. However a person who moves further along the path of submission, understanding, joyful acceptance and contentment, finds himself increasingly prepared for the next life. The next life will be as good as this phase of life, which is shaped according to our inner state and actions within the zone of time and space. If this life is based upon denials, quarrels, fears and anxieties, with no spiritual submission, all of this will be amplified in the next life. No change or escape will be possible then, for it is beyond space and time; it is eternal. The Fire there is eternal; here, one can step into or out of the fire. It is through the mercy of Allah that man comes to know the opposites – contentment and discontentment, certainty and doubt, knowledge and ignorance – so that he may choose the right path.

وَأَمَّا الَّذِينَ آمَنُوا وَعَمِلُوا الصَّالِحَاتِ فَيُوَفِّيهِمْ
أُجُورَهُمْ وَاللَّهُ لَا يُحِبُّ الظَّالِمِينَ

57 **And as for those who believe and do good deeds, He will compensate them fully. And Allah does not love the unjust.**

To describe the believers' reward Allah uses a word from the same root as the word used to describe Jesus' ascent to Him. Allah says in this verse that those who have trusted in Him have connected their belief to their actions. Faith (*īmān*, إيمان) cannot exist without correct actions (*al-a'māl al-ṣāliḥāt*, الأعمال الصالحات). For example, love for another person is unreal unless that love manifests itself in concern, attention and respect. Actions will prove intentions.

'And Allah does not love the unjust.' Allah has no love for the one who has transgressed or who has been unjust, and the highest injustice one can do is to one's self: 'We did not wrong them, but they wronged themselves' (2: 57). Creation is founded upon justice. If man does not maintain the balance, creation will rebound against him: the strength of that reaction depends on how far he has transgressed the bounds. It is obvious that we do not have an unlimited degree of freedom. We are bound by death and by the care we must observe over ourselves and our environment in order to maintain our individual and planetary health. Love and peace can only be founded and maintained upon the bedrock of justice.

ذَٰلِكَ نَتْلُوهُ عَلَيْكَ مِنَ الْآيَاتِ
وَالذِّكْرِ الْحَكِيمِ

58 **This We relate to you from among the signs and the wise remembrance.**

Here the Qur'an refers to its own revelation. In this verse, the Prophet Muhammad and his followers are told that the Qur'an is relating the story of the Prophet Jesus in order that they know the truth about Jesus and the events surrounding his life. The Prophet Muhammad had the truth conferred upon him so that he would be able to confront the Christians with it.

إِنَّ مَثَلَ عِيسَىٰ عِندَ اللَّهِ كَمَثَلِ آدَمَ خَلَقَهُ مِن تُرَابٍ
ثُمَّ قَالَ لَهُ كُن فَيَكُونُ

59 **Surely, the likeness of Jesus with Allah is as the likeness of Adam: He created him from dust, then said to him, Be! – and he was.**

The people of Nazareth used to say that because Jesus had no father, his father was Allah. The Qur'an addresses this mistaken claim by saying that Adam also had no father. So the example of the Prophet Jesus is the same as that of the Prophet Adam. Jesus had a physical reality: he was made of the same elements from which Allah created Adam and all creation. It challenges our intellect to accept the unusual situation of Jesus' birth, but logic will reveal to us that there cannot be a rule without an exception. In the case of Jesus' birth, the exception was part of divine mercy, because men's transgression had reached such a point that a direct, miraculous phenomenon had to interfere. That was Allah's decree. The event and its exceptional circumstance were intrinsic to rectifying the system.

If we abuse ourselves and divide our community, eventually that community or culture will be destroyed. We know of many such cases through examining archaeological remains. The arrogance and decadence of people caused their civilizations and cities to collapse. Allah's plot is perpetual, yet spontaneous; the forces it utilizes issue from within the system itself.

ٱلْحَقُّ مِن رَّبِّكَ فَلَا تَكُن مِّنَ ٱلْمُمْتَرِينَ

60 The truth is from your Lord, so do not be among those who doubt.

Man does not like doubt. What has been revealed concerning Jesus is the truth. There is also no doubt that the Prophet Muhammad had no doubt, as is revealed by the following verse.

فَمَنْ حَآجَّكَ فِيهِ مِنۢ بَعْدِ مَا جَآءَكَ مِنَ ٱلْعِلْمِ فَقُلْ
تَعَالَوْا۟ نَدْعُ أَبْنَآءَنَا وَأَبْنَآءَكُمْ وَنِسَآءَنَا وَنِسَآءَكُمْ
وَأَنفُسَنَا وَأَنفُسَكُمْ ثُمَّ نَبْتَهِلْ فَنَجْعَل لَّعْنَتَ
ٱللَّهِ عَلَى ٱلْكَٰذِبِينَ

61 So whoever disputes with you about this matter after the knowledge that has come to you, then say: Come, let us call our sons and your sons, our

women and your women, ourselves and yourselves, then let us be earnest in prayer and pray for the curse of Allah on those who lie.

The historical account of the event to which this verse refers is in most of the collections of sound (*ṣiḥāḥ*, صِحَاح) traditions from the Prophet, and also in the well-known Qur'anic commentaries (*tafāsīr*, تَفَاسِير). All the accounts are similar. The verse refers to a group of Christians from Najran in Yemen, who came with their leaders to the mosque of Medina using music and drums in the performance of their worship. Some of the Muslims came to the Prophet to protest; but to their surprise he told the Muslims to let them perform their religious rites. The next day there was to be a special event of the sort which took place whenever a disagreement could not be resolved. The men of that time were of such spiritual quality that they genuinely believed they had to delegate their problems to Allah. This was done by presenting their disagreements in the open before the entire community, when they would swear that if they were right or wrong, a sign should be sent to punish the wrongdoers. This was the last resort, when agreement could not be reached by the use of reasoning or conviction.

إِنَّ هَٰذَا لَهُوَ الْقَصَصُ الْحَقُّ ۚ وَمَا مِنْ إِلَٰهٍ إِلَّا اللَّهُ ۚ وَإِنَّ
اللَّهَ لَهُوَ الْعَزِيزُ الْحَكِيمُ

62 **Surely, this is the true account, and there is no god but Allah. Most surely, Allah is the Mighty, the Wise.**

In the Qur'an is the true story concerning Jesus and Mary. People who are not born with Arabic as their mother tongue have a great advantage over those who have been born native speakers of Arabic, because they must meet the language afresh and delve deeply into its linguistic meanings. Native speakers of

Arabic often take their language for granted, and interpret the Qur'an according to their superficial understanding of the language. For example, in this verse the word for 'account' (*qaṣaṣ*, قَصَص) also means 'narrative, tale', as well as 'clippings or cuttings'. 'To cut' (*qaṣṣa*, قَصَّ) is to make a differentiation. An account or narrative, therefore, stands out because it has been differentiated.

فَإِن تَوَلَّوْا فَإِنَّ اللَّهَ عَلِيمٌ بِالْمُفْسِدِينَ

63 **But if they turn back, then surely Allah knows those who corrupt.**

The truth is that there is no deity other than Allah, but most people do not accept anything other than their denial. 'To corrupt' (*fasada*, فَسَدَ) is the verbal root describing those who turn back. There is no corruption greater than the denial of truth.

قُلْ يَا أَهْلَ الْكِتَابِ تَعَالَوْا إِلَىٰ كَلِمَةٍ سَوَاءٍ بَيْنَنَا
وَبَيْنَكُمْ أَلَّا نَعْبُدَ إِلَّا اللَّهَ وَلَا نُشْرِكَ بِهِ شَيْئًا
وَلَا يَتَّخِذَ بَعْضُنَا بَعْضًا أَرْبَابًا مِّن دُونِ اللَّهِ
فَإِن تَوَلَّوْا فَقُولُوا اشْهَدُوا بِأَنَّا مُسْلِمُونَ

64 **Say: O followers of the Book! Let us come to an equitable proposition between us, that we shall not worship anything but Allah, that we shall not associate anything with Him, and that we shall not take others for lords besides Allah. Then if they turn away, say: Witness that we are among those who submit.**

This verse is said to have been directed at both the Christians of Najran and the Jews of Medina. Allah called upon the Jews and the Christians to accept a common denominator about which there were no differences, a denominator contained in their very own scriptures, the Torah and the Gospels. Allah called upon them to build on a united foundation, namely, not to worship any other than Allah and not to take another human being as Lord. Through the Prophet, Allah calls upon man to move according to what he inherently knows within himself. All the messengers of Reality said the same thing, as they all worshipped One God.

The people of unity (*tawḥīd*, تَوْحِيد) have singled themselves out by following the creed that 'there is no god but Allah and Muhammad is the messenger of Allah' (*lā ilāha illā Allāh wa Muḥammad rasūl Allāh*, لاَ إِلَهَ إِلاَّ اللهُ وَمُحَمد رَسُول الله) They accept all the prophets who came before. If other people are obstinate, the people of unity must announce their belief. After that – having done their best and having reached a point of differentiation (*furqān*, فُرْقَان) – they may say to the others, 'You have your way and I have mine' (109: 6). This is an assertion that there is no god in the form of man, so the trinity is rejected. No divine book has ever contained an utterance that there is any god except Allah.

يَٰٓأَهْلَ ٱلْكِتَٰبِ لِمَ تُحَآجُّونَ فِىٓ إِبْرَٰهِيمَ وَمَآ أُنزِلَتِ
ٱلتَّوْرَىٰةُ وَٱلْإِنجِيلُ إِلَّا مِنۢ بَعْدِهِۦٓ ۚ أَفَلَا تَعْقِلُونَ

65 **O People of the Book! Why do you dispute about Abraham, when the Torah and the Gospel were not revealed until after him? Have you no intellect?**

The Christians of Najran and the Jews of Medina disputed with the Prophet Muhammad about the legitimacy of Islam and the Qur'an in the light of their own beliefs. The Jews said that

Abraham was a Jew and the Christians said that he was a Christian. The Prophet Muhammad responded like all the messengers who brought books, saying that the purpose of creation is to understand and acknowledge 'Allah, there is no god but He, the Forever Living, the Eternal.' This is the first line of this chapter and it is the essence of the message carried by all prophets of the Adamic and Abrahamic lineage. 'Why do you dispute about Abraham?' He was neither a Jew nor a Christian as these terms are commonly understood. He was a prophet of submission, of Islam, Allah's true path.

Abraham and the messengers of all the divinely revealed religions were carriers of the same message, because there is in fact only one Reality. That message is that of submission to the one Creator, Allah, Who has revealed the meaning and purpose of creation repeatedly to His creation through His revealed books. Though the divine law has changed somewhat, the inner message in each book is the same. All these books contain the same meaning, but because of temporal circumstances, the outer laws have differed concerning what is forbidden and what is permitted, according to the time and the culture of the people. Every prophet accepted what had been revealed before him, acknowledging it and making it more relevant to his people's time and circumstances.

هَٰٓأَنتُمْ هَٰٓؤُلَآءِ حَٰجَجْتُمْ فِيمَا لَكُم بِهِۦ عِلْمٌ فَلِمَ
تُحَآجُّونَ فِيمَا لَيْسَ لَكُم بِهِۦ عِلْمٌ ۚ
وَٱللَّهُ يَعْلَمُ وَأَنتُمْ لَا تَعْلَمُونَ

66 **Behold! You disputed about that of which you had knowledge. Why then do you dispute about that of which you have no knowledge? And Allah knows while you do not know.**

The People of the Book argue and dispute amongst themselves according to their knowledge of the 'Book' of Judaism and Christianity, but it benefits no one to argue and dispute over knowledge which has been renewed and updated. Their knowledge is limited to what they have inherited. Real knowledge is with Allah and the last Messenger.

مَا كَانَ إِبْرَٰهِيمُ يَهُودِيًّا وَلَا نَصْرَانِيًّا وَلَٰكِن
كَانَ حَنِيفًا مُّسْلِمًا وَمَا كَانَ مِنَ الْمُشْرِكِينَ

67 **Abraham was not a Jew or a Christian, but he was [an] upright [man], one who submitted; and he was not among those who associate with Allah.**

The word translated as 'upright' (*ḥanīf*, حنيف) comes from a verb which means 'to turn' (*ḥanafa*, حنف) or 'to bend sideways, to bend away from that which is not straight'. Abraham bent away from that which was not right, implying that he was on a straight path. He was in Islam, in perfect submission, not associating partners with Allah. He was neither a Jew nor a Christian, as the People of the Book understand these terms today, but a man of Allah, inclining away from anything that deviated from the straight path to Reality.

إِنَّ أَوْلَى النَّاسِ بِإِبْرَٰهِيمَ لَلَّذِينَ اتَّبَعُوهُ وَهَٰذَا النَّبِيُّ
وَالَّذِينَ آمَنُوا وَاللَّهُ وَلِيُّ الْمُؤْمِنِينَ

68 **Surely, the nearest of people to Abraham are those who followed him and this Prophet and those who believe; and Allah is the guardian of the believers.**

'Nearest' (*awlā*, أولى) also means 'worthier, more entitled'. It is related to a word which means 'friend' (*walī*, ولي) and implies connectedness or closeness to Allah. Those who most deserve to belong to the way of Abraham are those who followed him, having imbibed his teaching and believed in his message. They include those who follow the Prophet Muhammad, for his teaching is an extension and expansion of the Abrahamic way. Generally, those who absorb the message of a prophet are those who are knowledgeable of its purpose and goal.

'And Allah is the guardian of the believers.' Allah is the guardian of those who embrace the true faith by recognizing His sovereignty (*wilāyah*, ولاية ; from the same root as *awlā* and *walī*). Allah is the Friend and Protector of each one of us, but we do not recognize that. Everyone, in actual fact, is in submission to Allah, but until that submission has become sacrosanct, recognized and translated into action, we are unified neither inwardly nor outwardly.

وَدَّت طَّآئِفَةٌ مِّنْ أَهْلِ ٱلْكِتَٰبِ لَوْ يُضِلُّونَكُمْ
وَمَا يُضِلُّونَ إِلَّآ أَنفُسَهُمْ وَمَا يَشْعُرُونَ

69 **A group of People of the Book desire to lead you astray. They lead no one astray but themselves, while they do not perceive.**

يَٰٓأَهْلَ ٱلْكِتَٰبِ لِمَ تَكْفُرُونَ بِـَٔايَٰتِ ٱللَّهِ
وَأَنتُمْ تَشْهَدُونَ

70 **O People of the Book! Why do you disbelieve in the signs of Allah while you witness them?**

The term 'People of the Book' refers specifically to the Jews who follow the Torah given to Moses and to the Christians who follow the Gospel given to Jesus. It is well known that the four accounts contained within the presently accepted New Testament were selected from a large number of similar narratives, almost all of which were compiled by people who had never seen the Prophet Jesus. There is no doubt that these books are personal interpretations and accounts, and not the words of Allah; contained within them are some truths along with some misinterpretations. Further doubt is cast upon the present New Testament because Jesus is known to have spoken Aramaic, the language of the land in which he dwelt, whereas the New Testament was originally written down in Greek.

The Qur'an stimulates the faculties of intelligence and reason to show the People of the Book that what they claim as true has been abrogated by the Qur'an. What is now in their hands in the form of the Qur'an contains what came before, and more. This is the primary message addressed to the People of the Book (*Ahl al-Kitāb,* أهل الكِتَاب). Allah, in the Qur'an, rhetorically asks why the People of the Book deny the signs of Allah that confirm the prophecy of Muhammad and the truthfulness of the Qur'an. If they had read their own books correctly, they would have come to recognize therein the promise of a final, perfect book for all mankind to follow.

يَا أَهْلَ الْكِتَابِ لِمَ تَلْبِسُونَ الْحَقَّ بِالْبَاطِلِ
وَتَكْتُمُونَ الْحَقَّ وَأَنْتُمْ تَعْلَمُونَ

71 O People of the Book! Why do you clothe the truth with falsehood and hide the truth while you know?

The People of the Book dress up (labisa, لَبِسَ) the truth even when they know it. They are in a state of hypocrisy, because they know what is right and what is wrong.

وَقَالَتْ طَّآئِفَةٌ مِّنْ أَهْلِ ٱلْكِتَٰبِ ءَامِنُوا۟ بِٱلَّذِىٓ أُنزِلَ عَلَى ٱلَّذِينَ
ءَامَنُوا۟ وَجْهَ ٱلنَّهَارِ وَٱكْفُرُوٓا۟ ءَاخِرَهُۥ لَعَلَّهُمْ يَرْجِعُونَ

72 **And a party of the People of the Book say at the beginning of the day: Believe in that which has been revealed to those who believe; then, at the end of the day they disbelieve that perhaps they may return.**

Some of the People of the Book took the way of Allah at their own convenience and desired only to appease the Muslims. One of the inward meanings of this verse is that the first part of the day, when light appears, is a metaphor for the confrontation with truth, from which there is no escape. When the sun is up, man must accept what he sees. When darkness sets in again, however, doubts may return.

This verse describes the plight of one who doubts. His heart is not established in the right place, and he vacillates. Only when he is confronted with the inescapable truth does he accept it; however, if the slightest opposition within him arises, he will return to his doubts. As a result of these doubts, he is in a profoundly unsettled state. Yet no one wants to be uncertain and insecure; we all seek to know and experience the security of certainty.

وَلَا تُؤْمِنُوٓا إِلَّا لِمَن تَبِعَ دِينَكُمْ قُلْ إِنَّ ٱلْهُدَىٰ هُدَى ٱللَّهِ
أَن يُؤْتَىٰٓ أَحَدٌ مِّثْلَ مَآ أُوتِيتُمْ أَوْ يُحَآجُّوكُمْ
عِندَ رَبِّكُمْ قُلْ إِنَّ ٱلْفَضْلَ بِيَدِ ٱللَّهِ
يُؤْتِيهِ مَن يَشَآءُ
وَٱللَّهُ وَٰسِعٌ عَلِيمٌ

73 Believe only in one who follows your religion. Say: Surely, the true guidance is the guidance of Allah, that one may be given [by Him] the like of what you were given, or that they would contend with you in the presence of your Lord. Say: Surely, the bounty is in Allah's hand. He gives it to whom He pleases, and Allah possesses vast knowledge.

Man desires confirmation of his beliefs, therefore he wants to be in an environment in which his habits are shared by the majority. For example, people who smoke prefer to do so with other smokers because they seek confirmation and acceptance of this habit. Those who share common values club together to enhance those values and establish them more deeply within their existing life pattern. When confronted with someone who differs from them, they feel that their security is threatened. They fear that their beliefs may be changed through such a confrontation. To retain one's security in the face of an ever-changing world, one must trust in Allah, and trust that all one chooses in good faith will be for one's ultimate good.

At first glance this verse and the previous one look like the dissimulation (*taqīyyah*, تقيّة) practised when necessary by the

Muslims. The difference is that the Muslim does not contradict his knowledge although he may hide it (though only for a while) from those who cannot accept it. Artificial codes of behaviour other than Islam are systems merely for appeasement and expedience. It is incumbent upon every Muslim to speak the truth. Silence prevails only if a person knows that the situation will overcome him because he is not strong enough to stand up to the results of his pronouncements. Also, our pronouncements must not be mere criticisms or judgements which result from our personal opinions. If one is certain of the truth of one's convictions, then one's duty is to propagate them.

Nobody can come to Islam unless their heart turns toward the truth. With this turning, one will begin to experience complete freedom from one's self-imposed veils and prejudices, and will be guided by the heart. That is the true path to Islam. Joy and blessedness are for every human being who has the potential to see nothing other than the glory of Allah's perfection in creation, and to move toward his or her own perfection.

'Say: Surely, the true guidance is the guidance of Allah.' Allah will guide those who have true, secure trust and faith. Whoever has that trust and faith (*īmān*, إيمان) confirmed in him will never deviate from the path, nor will he give it up. The more he is afflicted, the more he will see the perfect laws of the Creator, even at the cost of personal suffering.

'Say: Surely, the bounty is in Allah's hand.' One who seeks the bounty or grace of Allah will surely receive it, provided one seeks it while being willing to give up all that one has. The process begins when a person gives up something that dissatisfies him. We cannot step on to a train heading in a new direction unless we step off the one we are on now; some people try to be on two trains at once, which is not possible. We must give up falsehood before the truth will come to us.

'He gives it to whom He pleases.' The Qur'an is the subtlest of teachers. Though under Allah's will, man must nevertheless develop his intellect, for by using reason and logic he eventually draws so close to Allah that his will becomes Allah's. Drawing close to Allah is no mere mental act, nor is it pure inspiration; but it begins with the intellect through the tethering of reason.

يَخْتَصُّ بِرَحْمَتِهِ مَن يَشَآءُ ۗ
وَاللَّهُ ذُو الْفَضْلِ الْعَظِيمِ

74 **He specially chooses for His mercy whom He pleases; and Allah possesses great bounty.**

To see the pervasive nature of mercy (*raḥmah*, رَحْمَة) is to receive the great bounty of Allah. If one really wants to know the Book, one will certainly come to know it. Many Muslims today think that because they were born into a Muslim family, they automatically have a deeper understanding of the Qur'an than those who were not. But 'Ali said, 'You are the evident book. By your hidden signs the secret becomes evident.' If the reading of Allah's written Book, the Qur'an, does not lead them to uncover and absorb their own inner book, then the written book will not have been read and absorbed.

وَمِنْ أَهْلِ الْكِتَابِ مَنْ إِن تَأْمَنْهُ بِقِنطَارٍ يُؤَدِّهِ إِلَيْكَ
وَمِنْهُم مَّنْ إِن تَأْمَنْهُ بِدِينَارٍ لَّا يُؤَدِّهِ إِلَيْكَ إِلَّا مَا دُمْتَ
عَلَيْهِ قَآئِمًا ۗ ذَٰلِكَ بِأَنَّهُمْ قَالُوا لَيْسَ عَلَيْنَا فِي الْأُمِّيِّينَ سَبِيلٌ
وَيَقُولُونَ عَلَى اللَّهِ الْكَذِبَ وَهُمْ يَعْلَمُونَ

75 **And among the People of the Book are some who will return a treasury full of wealth if you entrust it to them. Others will not pay back a dinar unless you**

continually demand it from them. This is because they say: We are not obliged (to be honest) with illiterate people. They knowingly speak lies about Allah while they know the truth.

A *dīnār* (دينار) was a large coin made of gold: its paper equivalent of that name is still used in the Middle East. The origin of the word is 'home of fire' (*dār al-nār,* دار النار), because love of money is a source of increasing trouble. Unless people are constantly reminded, few will honour their agreements more than rarely.

The credit systems of today take full advantage of man's greed. The feeling of not having to pay for something immediately, coupled with the belief, encouraged by retailers, that their products are desirable, if not necessary, causes people to buy more and more. Individual and governmental debt increases, based upon the false notion that economic growth has no limit. But people of knowledge warn about such false notions. Every creational system is subject to cyclical growth and decline and has its limits. Veiled from the truth by his greed for material security, man arrogantly supposes that he will circumvent the inevitable downward cycle, and by this very arrogance he increases his carelessness and hastens his ultimate fall.

This verse unequivocally explains man's rationalization of his injustice to his fellow man. He reasons that the goal of life is the acquisition of material goods, and uses his knowledge to subjugate others less aware and more vulnerable.

بَلَىٰ مَنْ أَوْفَىٰ بِعَهْدِهِۦ وَٱتَّقَىٰ فَإِنَّ ٱللَّهَ يُحِبُّ ٱلْمُتَّقِينَ

76 Allah loves whoever fulfils his promise and guards carefully against wrong action.

Everyone must fulfil his promises, as long as these were not extracted under duress. Difference of religion must not be used to justify greed. The teaching of the Qur'an helps us to recognize and control our greed.

إِنَّ الَّذِينَ يَشْتَرُونَ بِعَهْدِ اللَّهِ وَأَيْمَانِهِمْ ثَمَنًا
قَلِيلًا أُولَٰئِكَ لَا خَلَاقَ لَهُمْ فِي الْآخِرَةِ
وَلَا يُكَلِّمُهُمُ اللَّهُ وَلَا يَنظُرُ إِلَيْهِمْ يَوْمَ الْقِيَامَةِ
وَلَا يُزَكِّيهِمْ وَلَهُمْ عَذَابٌ أَلِيمٌ

77 **As for those who exchange their pledges to Allah for a small price, surely, they shall have no portion in the Hereafter, and Allah will not speak to them, nor will He look upon them on the Day of Resurrection. He will not purify them, and they shall have a painful chastisement.**

Those who exchange their submission and love for Allah for worldly power or wealth, or any other such distraction, are at a loss. Their share of this world is bound to be very small and in the Hereafter they are doomed. The man of Allah takes what he needs from this world in order to prepare himself for the next.

Man's forgetfulness makes him address only rarely the vital questions of the meaning of life, such as why it ends and what comes next. And yet he fears death and the unknown to come.

What does 'Allah will not speak to them' mean? Silence is often used as a sign of conflict or disconnection, because it indicates that there is no relationship between the two parties concerned. Those to whom it appears Allah does not speak have no relationship with Reality, for in their lives they have cultivated no relationship with truth. Though the entire message of life concerns the oneness of the Creator Who has created all things and Who sustains them through His grace, they were not connected with this message. Everything – every seen or unseen creational manifestation – is permeated by the eternal power of that Reality. If Allah does not speak to us, it is because we have turned a deaf ear to Him.

We have to prepare ourselves in this life to be ready for the next. Pure actions have their rewards here and now. Even if one hesitates over belief in a next life, logic clearly reveals that one who follows Allah's indicated path will be given everything needed in this life as well as the next.

وَإِنَّ مِنْهُمْ لَفَرِيقًا يَلْوُنَ أَلْسِنَتَهُم بِالْكِتَابِ لِتَحْسَبُوهُ
مِنَ الْكِتَابِ وَمَا هُوَ مِنَ الْكِتَابِ وَيَقُولُونَ هُوَ مِنْ عِندِ اللَّهِ
وَمَا هُوَ مِنْ عِندِ اللَّهِ وَيَقُولُونَ عَلَى اللَّهِ الْكَذِبَ
وَهُمْ يَعْلَمُونَ

78 **Most surely there exists a party amongst them who recite the Book in order that you may consider it to be from the Book; but it is not from the Book. They say it is from Allah, while it is not from Allah; and they lie about Allah even though they know the truth.**

Often the Qur'an or a tradition is taken out of its context and thus distorted or limited, or even rendered meaningless. For example, part of a tradition says, 'Allah has created Adam in His form.' But are we in the form of Allah? Taken out of context, this tradition is confusing, because the Qur'an says, 'There is nothing like Him' (112: 4). How can a tradition contradict the Qur'an, and how can it be said that man is like Allah? The tradition comes from an incident in which the Prophet overheard two men quarrelling; one of them cursed the other, saying, 'The curse of Allah be upon you and everybody who is like you.' The Prophet turned to that man and said, 'Do not say this. Allah has created Adam in his form', meaning in the form of the man that he was cursing, not in the form of Allah!

Another example of a frequently used tradition which leads to much misunderstanding when not quoted in its entirety is this: 'Marriage is half of the life-transaction (*dīn,* دين).' This tradition concludes with the phrase, 'So that you may complete the other half.' That is to say, we can pay attention to the other, more important half, the spiritual half, of ourselves by challenging our physical and human needs through marriage. By marrying, we free ourselves to devote our attention to other requirements which are subtler and higher.

'And they say it is from Allah while it is not from Allah.' Everything is from Allah, including the freedom to forget partial truths, a freedom which will imprison a man more and more within the domain of his self-constructed fantasy. It is in man's nature to find evidence to support himself in fulfilling his desires; therefore he must always be on guard not to twist the truth, and interpret according to his own whim.

Man brings about injustice through his covetousness and greed, for he is able to justify to himself every action and make it seem attractive. Even the act of murder is attractive to the murderer, because he is so desirous of attaining his goal that he can justify his own violence. It is in the nature of the mind and the ego to concoct partial truths and lies, but to propagate a lie against Allah is to distort the perception of reality within the creational experience, and to ignore the criteria established by Allah.

مَا كَانَ لِبَشَرٍ أَنْ يُؤْتِيَهُ اللّٰهُ الْكِتَابَ وَالْحُكْمَ
وَالنُّبُوَّةَ ثُمَّ يَقُولَ لِلنَّاسِ كُونُوا عِبَادًا لِّي مِنْ
دُونِ اللّٰهِ وَلٰكِنْ كُونُوا رَبَّانِيِّينَ بِمَا كُنْتُمْ تُعَلِّمُونَ
الْكِتَابَ وَبِمَا كُنْتُمْ تَدْرُسُونَ

79 It is not possible that Allah would give a mortal the Book, wisdom, and the prophethood, and then that mortal would say to other men: Serve me instead of Allah. Rather, [he would say]: Worship the Lord, because you study and teach the Book.

The Qur'an refers here to the Prophet Jesus, explaining that it is impossible for a prophet, a man selected by Allah because of his purity and wisdom and one who has been given the Book, to order his people to worship him. How could he tell them anything other than 'Be worshippers of the Lord'?

The word 'to study' (*darasa*, دَرَسَ) as used in this verse also means 'to wipe out, to obliterate'. By studying something very carefully, one can obliterate all traces of ignorance concerning it. Man is born in order to obliterate ignorance within him, for once ignorance is destroyed, knowledge appears. Obliterate darkness and light will appear. Obliterate the impulse which causes us to remain in ignorance and distraction from the remembrance of Allah (*ghaflah*, غَفْلَة), and we will enter into the effulgent light of awareness and knowledge.

وَلَا يَأْمُرَكُمْ أَنْ تَتَّخِذُوا الْمَلَائِكَةَ وَالنَّبِيِّينَ
أَرْبَابًا أَيَأْمُرُكُمْ بِالْكُفْرِ بَعْدَ إِذْ أَنْتُمْ مُسْلِمُونَ

80 **Neither would he enjoin that you take the angels and the prophets as lords. Would he enjoin unbelief upon you when you are people of submission?**

No man of knowledge, and certainly no Prophet, would tell us to take the angels or messengers as Lords. How could such beings encourage others to deny, by the very affirmation of unity (*tawḥīd*, تَوحِيد), the one and only Truth? This verse describes submission as the way to unity. The way to the understanding of unity in its universal sense is the path of submission and adherence to its laws.

وَإِذْ أَخَذَ اللَّهُ مِيثَاقَ النَّبِيِّينَ لَمَا آتَيْتُكُمْ مِنْ
كِتَابٍ وَحِكْمَةٍ ثُمَّ جَاءَكُمْ رَسُولٌ مُصَدِّقٌ لِمَا
مَعَكُمْ لَتُؤْمِنُنَّ بِهِ وَلَتَنْصُرُنَّهُ قَالَ أَأَقْرَرْتُمْ وَأَخَذْتُمْ
عَلَىٰ ذَٰلِكُمْ إِصْرِي قَالُوا أَقْرَرْنَا قَالَ فَاشْهَدُوا
وَأَنَا مَعَكُمْ مِنَ الشَّاهِدِينَ

81 **Allah made a covenant with the prophets: Behold, I have given you the Book and wisdom. Then a messenger came, verifying what was with you. Believe in him and aid him. He said: Do you affirm and accept Allah's covenant in this matter? They said: Yes, we affirm. He said: Then bear witness, and I will bear witness with you.**

Alī commented about this verse, 'Allah did not send a prophet without making a covenant (*'ahd*, عهد) with him.' And in the Qur'an the Prophet Jesus says, 'I give you the good news that there will be a Prophet coming after me' (61: 6). In the New Testament (John 14: 16) Jesus says, 'And I shall pray to the Father, and He will give you another comforter, that he may abide with you forever.'

All the prophets were given the essence of knowledge, and knowledge of essence, and it is impossible that this total view lacked the knowledge that their systems of divine law were as yet incomplete. The process of unfolding the fullness of divine law throughout time is similar to bringing up a child: what he is instructed to do at the age of six will be changed when he reaches the age of fifteen. Moses tightened what was lax in the Law; Jesus revived the spirit of the Law. Any increase in the restrictions that the prophets brought was in essence an increase of real freedom to the followers of the path of submission, because as the path became more clearly defined the chance of going astray decreased.

All the Prophets took the covenant (*iṣr*, إصر) and bore witness to it; yet the fact remains that most Jews and Christians do not accept this. Man usually seeks to remain a passive slave to his habits and inherited customs; he rarely makes the effort to shake himself loose from what binds him. It is easy to shirk the responsibility for his intellect and power of reason.

فَمَنْ تَوَلَّىٰ بَعْدَ ذَٰلِكَ فَأُولَٰئِكَ هُمُ الْفَاسِقُونَ

82 So whoever turns back after this is a transgressor.

اَفَغَيْرَ دِينِ اللّٰهِ يَبْغُونَ وَلَهُۥٓ اَسْلَمَ مَنْ فِى السَّمٰوٰتِ
وَالْاَرْضِ طَوْعًا وَكَرْهًا وَاِلَيْهِ يُرْجَعُونَ

83 **Do they seek to follow other than Allah's way when whatever is in the heavens and the earth submit to Him willingly or unwillingly, and to Him all will return.**

How can it be that anyone wants other than the way of Allah when all things in the heavens and earth, willingly or unwillingly, submit to Him? The secret of submission lies in recognizing and understanding the will of the Creator. Once this is done, it is possible to know the correct direction of travel and to know how to use one's individual will in accordance with the multitudinous laws of this existence. When we truly perceive the laws that govern this existence, we will not desire what is not in line with the Creator's will, and therefore we will meet with nothing but success. When one's will submits to the decree of Reality, one has truly attained freedom. Then one fully recognizes the laboratory of life, and discovers through disappointment and failure what follows the line of the Creator's will. The person who meets with his failures before the end of his life is very fortunate, because through failure he is able to discover what is wrong.

The greater the spiritual aspiration of a man, the greater is his affliction. Ultimately, through continued learning from suffering, the only affliction that will remain is that which is the result of others' ignorance and heedlessness. What higher affliction could there be than the suffering of the Prophet Jesus when he saw the ignorance and resistance that enveloped the people around him? It is a tremendous affliction for a teacher to find that the people around him are not interested in learning, just as it is an affliction for a father to find that his children are not responding to his love, care and attention. Knowledge is power, but it cannot be imposed on others. Every heart, every individual, must want it, for if it is not desired it can never be obtained. Once desired, its acquisition becomes easy. Ultimately, a time will come when every being in existence will have united his will with the will of the Creator. At that time peace will prevail on the earth. There can be no peace on earth while man seeks anxiously to justify his wrong actions. Peace and love need justice.

قُلْ آمَنَّا بِاللَّهِ وَمَا أُنْزِلَ عَلَيْنَا وَمَا أُنْزِلَ عَلَىٰ إِبْرَاهِيمَ
وَإِسْمَاعِيلَ وَإِسْحَاقَ وَيَعْقُوبَ وَالْأَسْبَاطِ وَمَا
أُوتِيَ مُوسَىٰ وَعِيسَىٰ وَالنَّبِيُّونَ مِنْ رَبِّهِمْ
لَا نُفَرِّقُ بَيْنَ أَحَدٍ مِنْهُمْ وَنَحْنُ لَهُ مُسْلِمُونَ

84 **Say: We believe in Allah and what has been revealed to us, and what was revealed to Abraham, Ishmael, Isaac, Jacob, and the tribes; and what was given to Moses, Jesus, and the prophets from their Lord. We make no distinction between any of them, and to Him do we submit.**

The command is for all who believe in Allah – the unitarians, the followers of the Prophet Muhammad, and the true followers of all the prophets – to say, 'We believe in reality, we believe in Allah and what has descended upon us, in what we found in our heart. We believe in all the prophets without differentiation (as to their standing with Allah).' In our ignorance we differentiate between the prophets. Culturally, linguistically and historically, each people's messenger differs from the others, but essentially they are all the same, for the message they bring is the timeless, divine message of submission and awakening to the truth. This verse reaffirms that Muhammad confirmed everything that had gone before him, while pointing out the areas which had become corrupted or needed clarification or updating.

The religion of the Prophet Abraham was Islam and the followers of Abraham were Muslims. The religion of the Prophet Moses was also Islam, but later named Judaism. At the time of Jesus, again, Islam as Judaism was revived as Christianity and later distorted and confused. Islam is Allah's unique path and message, but appears historically as different religions. In reality they are part of one continuum in the spiritual evolution of man.

The Qur'an calls upon us to open our eyes so that we do not fall into the trap of dispute and argumentation (*jidāl,* جِدَال). 'There is no argument concerning the path to Allah' (*la jidāl fī al-dīn,* لا جِدال في الدين), the Prophetic tradition says. There can be no argument because there is only one truth, which leads to itself via itself. The path is from Allah, to Allah, via Allah. Through struggle we become the instrument of Allah realizing that all action is from Him and that there is no permanent reality other than Him. As man dives deeper within himself he finds that there is no end to the inner domain, because the end is the other side of the beginning. Allah is the First, Allah is the Last; all creation has emanated from Allah, is sustained by Him, and returns to Him.

Man must reflect. He will gain freedom, and will understand its meaning only by reflecting upon and truly recognizing his constriction. Should he then be placed in a tiny prison-cell, he would still remain free within his soul. To use one's intellect is to work within creational limitations. Man's spirit is a reflector of the entire truth.

وَمَن يَبْتَغِ غَيْرَ الْإِسْلَامِ دِينًا فَلَن يُقْبَلَ مِنْهُ
وَهُوَ فِي الْآخِرَةِ مِنَ الْخَاسِرِينَ

85 And whoever desires a religion other than Islam, it

shall not be accepted from him, and in the Hereafter he shall be among the losers.

Whoever seeks another path other than submission to Allah and struggle in the way of Allah is already at a loss. Since there is no possibility for action in the next life, there is no possibility for change. One will therefore be in a state of total loss. This life is given to us in order to complete and fashion the self through our actions. With death comes the end of the process of self-unfolding.

كَيْفَ يَهْدِي اللَّهُ قَوْمًا كَفَرُوا بَعْدَ إِيمَانِهِمْ
وَشَهِدُوا أَنَّ الرَّسُولَ حَقٌّ وَجَاءَهُمُ الْبَيِّنَاتُ
وَاللَّهُ لَا يَهْدِي الْقَوْمَ الظَّالِمِينَ

86 **How shall Allah guide a people who disbelieved after their belief; and they had borne witness that the messenger was true: clear arguments had come to them. Allah does not guide the unjust people.**

With each prophet there were followers who, even after they had come to recognize the truth of the message, failed to follow it. How can Reality guide a person who turns away from truth after being shown it, and who then returns to heedlessness? Once a man has known something to be true, he is at an even greater loss if he does not act upon his knowledge. If the knowledge which he has been given is not used properly, his life becomes even more difficult than it was before. Having received knowledge, one is then accountable for it; for this reason Allah does not question the people who have not received the message.

أُولَٰٓئِكَ جَزَآؤُهُمْ أَنَّ عَلَيْهِمْ لَعْنَةَ ٱللَّهِ
وَٱلْمَلَٰٓئِكَةِ وَٱلنَّاسِ أَجْمَعِينَ

87 Their reward is the curse of Allah upon them and the curse of the angels and of mankind all together.

The recompense for unjust people is a true curse of affliction, turmoil and sorrow. The angels (*al-malā' ikah*, الملائِكة) are those unseen forces continuously at work in nature. We realize that millions of energy bands exist, about which man knows very little. We do not really know what the force of gravity is, for example, or how it works. We say that two bodies are attracted through magnetic forces, but we cannot explain – beyond a physical description – what magnetism is. We could say that this attraction is the action of unseen energies called angels. The word for angel in Arabic (*malak*, مَلَك) derives from a root which means 'power', for angelic entities are part of the power that governs existence.

خَٰلِدِينَ فِيهَا لَا يُخَفَّفُ عَنْهُمُ ٱلْعَذَابُ
وَلَا هُمْ يُنظَرُونَ

88 Abiding in it forever; their chastisement shall not be lightened and they shall not be given respite.

In the next realm of existence there is no time, therefore there can be no change in a person's state.

إِلَّا الَّذِينَ تَابُوا مِنْ بَعْدِ ذَٰلِكَ وَأَصْلَحُوا
فَإِنَّ اللَّهَ غَفُورٌ رَحِيمٌ

89 **Except those who repent after that and amend; then surely, Allah is Forgiving, Merciful.**

It is related in a tradition that one of the early followers of the Prophet Muhammad later turned against him, taking others away with him. Eventually some of them returned. If one looks for what appear to be faults in a prophet or in any human being, one will find them; if one wishes to see the unity and perfection of Allah's laws, then one will also see that.

There is no point having knowledge unless it can be applied, unless it brings about restoration and reparation (*iṣlāḥ*, إِصْلاَح), unless it serves to put right what is wrong. We can only question each other about our actions, not our intentions, knowing that in time our actions and intentions will be unified. Eventually, our intentions will be made known. We must therefore be steadfast and seek to amend.

'By the time, surely man is in loss' (103: 1-2). Man is always at a loss because of his lower, animal nature: if he allows it to prevail, it will. Only those who believe recognize that they are born in order to perfect themselves. In order to do that they translate their belief into correct actions (*'amilū al-ṣaliḥāt*, عَمِلُوا الصَّالِحَات): 'Then surely Allah is Forgiving, Merciful.' Allah will always provide for us generously if we turn towards Him.

إِنَّ الَّذِينَ كَفَرُوا بَعْدَ إِيمَانِهِمْ ثُمَّ ازْدَادُوا كُفْرًا
لَنْ تُقْبَلَ تَوْبَتُهُمْ وَأُولَٰئِكَ هُمُ الضَّالُّونَ

90 **Surely, those who disbelieve after their belief, then**

increase in unbelief, their repentance shall not be accepted. They are among the ones who go astray.

This is a historical reference to the Children of Israel. They were at a loss before Moses came to them, believing in the message that he brought but returning nevertheless to disbelief. Eventually, they rejected the last messenger to come to them – Jesus. 'Their repentance shall not be accepted.' Those of us who catch a glimpse of truth are reminded that there must be an everlasting Truth. Covering or denying its light only serves to increase our darkness and ignorance.

إِنَّ ٱلَّذِينَ كَفَرُوا۟ وَمَاتُوا۟ وَهُمْ كُفَّارٌ فَلَن يُقْبَلَ
مِنْ أَحَدِهِم مِّلْءُ ٱلْأَرْضِ ذَهَبًا وَلَوِ ٱفْتَدَىٰ بِهِۦٓ
أُو۟لَٰٓئِكَ لَهُمْ عَذَابٌ أَلِيمٌ وَمَا لَهُم
مِّن نَّٰصِرِينَ

91 **Even if those who disbelieve and die while they are non-believers should wish to ransom themselves with all the gold in the earth, the ransom would not be accepted from any of them. They shall have a painful chastisement, and they shall have no helpers.**

To die in a state of denial and darkness is to lose any chance of reaching light. Only now, in this world, can man save himself. Attachment to this life blinds man to the fact that he is really free and that this life, this journey from birth to death, is not something to cling to. He alone can unwrap the cocoon of desires which he has woven around himself. 'Allah does not change the condition of a people until they change their own condition' (13: 11). Allah also says, 'And they did not do Us any harm, but they wronged their own souls' (16: 118).

لَن تَنَالُوا الْبِرَّ حَتَّىٰ تُنفِقُوا مِمَّا تُحِبُّونَ ۚ وَمَا تُنفِقُوا
مِن شَيْءٍ فَإِنَّ اللَّهَ بِهِ عَلِيمٌ

92 By no means shall you attain to righteousness until you spend of what you love; and whatever you spend, Allah surely knows it.

The word translated here as 'righteousness' (*birr*, بِرّ) also means 'piety, devoutness'. It is closely connected to another word which means 'an expanse of land, desert (*barr*, بَرّ). Everyone wants expansion and freedom. We will never be able to receive our reward unless we first expand beyond our limitations by spending (*infāq*, إنفاق) giving freely from what we love. We cannot reach a state of righteousness unless we renounce our attachments. Freedom can be attained only when the most important thing for us is our state of true submission. Possessions and worldly things are a test by which we can measure our degree of freedom or bondage. Are goods and services our slaves, to be put to use for our higher aspirations, or are we in fact their slaves, devoting all our thought and attention to them?

كُلُّ الطَّعَامِ كَانَ حِلًّا لِّبَنِي إِسْرَائِيلَ إِلَّا مَا حَرَّمَ إِسْرَائِيلُ
عَلَىٰ نَفْسِهِ مِن قَبْلِ أَن تُنَزَّلَ التَّوْرَاةُ ۗ قُلْ فَأْتُوا
بِالتَّوْرَاةِ فَاتْلُوهَا إِن كُنتُمْ صَادِقِينَ

93 All food was lawful to the Children of Israel except what Israel had forbidden to himself before the

Torah was revealed. Say: Bring the Torah then, and recite it if you are truthful.

This verse is a historical reference to the Prophet Jacob, the son of Isaac, who was also known as Israel. One of the objections that the Jews of Medina raised against the Prophet Muhammad was that Islam made it permissible to eat most of the meats considered forbidden by the Jews, in particular, camel's meat. The Jews included Jacob's personal preferences in their interpretation of Judaic law. It may have been that Jacob did not eat the meat of camels; in some traditions it is mentioned that he could not digest camel's meat, but for whatever reason, he did not eat certain foods. The Prophet Muhammad also abstained from some foods such as garlic, and some people have tried to follow these habits blindly, though on several occasions the Prophet is reported to have given garlic to someone to eat because of its therapeutic qualities. The Prophet explained that though he did not eat garlic, it had certain beneficial properties for people.

The Family of 'Imrān is a very detailed and comprehensive chapter of the Qur'an, permeated entirely with (*tawḥid,* تَوحيد), unity, the Oneness of Allah. This verse, and a few others like it, indicates the importance of research and reasoning. It is not in man's nature to accept blindly what is given to him. Though he may begin his journey with blind faith, his certainty is gradually confirmed by reason and knowledge.

فَمَنِ افْتَرَىٰ عَلَى اللَّهِ الْكَذِبَ مِنْ بَعْدِ ذَٰلِكَ
فَأُولَٰئِكَ هُمُ الظَّالِمُونَ

94 **Whoever fabricates a lie against Allah after this is unjust.**

The power of reasoning awakens. If the clear signs of Allah

are shown to us and we persist in denying Him, we are nothing other than our own oppressors (*ẓālimūn*, ظالمون). If we continue to bury the truth within ourselves we do ourselves great injustice, and no growth can take place. If through the use of the intellect there is no increase in self-knowledge, one will find nothing but darkness. As a person who has never developed his intellect and reason grows older, he regresses to a childlike state. Whoever has used his intellect vigorously, on the other hand, is enhanced by the passing years, for his knowledge and wisdom have continually increased.

قُلْ صَدَقَ اللَّهُ فَاتَّبِعُوا مِلَّةَ إِبْرَاهِيمَ حَنِيفًا
وَمَا كَانَ مِنَ الْمُشْرِكِينَ

95 **Say: Allah has spoken the truth, so follow the way of Abraham, the upright one; he was not one of those who associate with Allah.**

The Qur'an continues to clarify that the Prophet Jacob did not introduce a rule which proscribed the eating of those things forbidden by Jewish law. The Qur'an says, 'Say: Allah has spoken the truth.' The Qur'an is a continuation of the creed of Abraham: 'And he was not one of those who associate with Allah.' The message in the Qur'an merely completes the message of the previous prophets, including Abraham, Jacob, Moses and Jesus.

إِنَّ أَوَّلَ بَيْتٍ وُضِعَ لِلنَّاسِ لَلَّذِي بِبَكَّةَ
مُبَارَكًا وَهُدًى لِلْعَالَمِينَ

96 **Surely, the first house appointed for men is the one at Bakkah, blessed, and a guidance for all nations.**

It is known that there were other houses of worship built

before the Ka'bah in Mecca, but the Ka'bah was built for all nations, not for one particular family or community. (*Bakkah* (بَكَّة) is another name for Mecca. It is the plot of land upon which the Ka'bah stands, while Mecca is the town and market-place. Ba'kkah is very similar in form to the verb which means 'to grieve, cry, lament' (*bakā*, بَكَى). Crying is the door which opens humbled hearts to worship. It is recommended to weep when reading the Qur'an, for it softens the heart and loosens the ties which bind us to this physical existence.

فِيهِ آيَاتٌ بَيِّنَاتٌ مَقَامُ إِبْرَاهِيمَ ۖ وَمَنْ دَخَلَهُ كَانَ آمِنًا ۗ
وَلِلَّهِ عَلَى النَّاسِ حِجُّ الْبَيْتِ مَنِ اسْتَطَاعَ إِلَيْهِ سَبِيلًا ۚ
وَمَنْ كَفَرَ فَإِنَّ اللَّهَ غَنِيٌّ عَنِ الْعَالَمِينَ

97 In it are clear signs: [it is] the Station of Abraham, and whoever enters it shall be secure. Pilgrimage to the House is incumbent upon men for the sake of Allah, [upon] everyone who is able to undertake the journey to it. And whoever disbelieves, then surely Allah is Self-Sufficient, beyond any need of the creation.

Once a person has entered a state of abandonment and peace, he has entered the House of Allah and complete safety. The Qur'an enjoins us to ensure that Bakkah remains a sanctuary. Even pre-Islamic practices prohibited any person or living creature from being harmed there; it was forbidden even to harm a louse. The outer sanctuary must be established and maintained before the inner sanctuary can be attained.

Originally built by Abraham, the Ka'bah is a cuboid structure ten by twelve metres, reaching a height of sixteen metres. It has a door positioned in one corner, which is two metres in height.

The Black Stone, set into the corner nearest the door, is a piece of meteorite. The House has been rebuilt many times. The northern corner of the house is called the Iraqi corner, the western corner is called the Syrian corner, the southern is called the Yemeni, and the eastern corner, where the stone is found, is called the Stone (*al-Ḥajar*, الحَجَر). The walls of the Ka'bah were much lower at the time when the Prophet returned to Mecca in victory. He went to the Ka'bah and removed the idols that were hanging upon the walls by lifting 'Alī upon his shoulders, so that he could remove the highest ones. If the House of Allah had been as tall then as it is today, he could never have reached the top in this manner.

The Ka'bah has always been covered with cloth to commemorate the first cover which Hagar had placed upon the door. For centuries new cloth was added, but the old pieces were never removed; until one of the Abbāsid rulers ordered that the cloth be taken down, for the House was on the verge of collapse from the excessive weight. About 800 years ago the decision was made that the cloth be replaced every year. From the time of the Prophet Muhammad, women could pray anywhere within the sanctuary of the Sacred Mosque which surrounded the Ka'bah; there was no segregation according to gender.

The Ka'bah has had a number of guardians. Two major tribes occupied the area until the time of Qusayy ibn Kilab, that is, 200 years before the Prophet's emigration to Medina. One of the Prophet Muhammad's great-grandfathers renovated it after it had been burnt to the ground. From Qusayy, the guardianship of the Ka'bah was handed down to the sons of Hashim from the tribe of Quraysh. It was a great honour to be guardian of the Ancient House of worship. People of many different religions came to it from all over the world. It was also a major centre of trade, as Mecca was the midpoint on the route from Yemen to Damascus.

During the rule of Yazīd, toward the end of the seventh century A.D., a battle was fought in Mecca. The sanctuary was ransacked and the walls of the Ka'bah were pulled down. The Ka'bah was later rebuilt in the same location. At that time, sixty years after the Migration (*Hijrah*, هِجْرَة), the House had two doors, and the inside, like the outside, was covered with cloth. It is related that the mother of Abbas, the Prophet's uncle, made a vow to give birth to a man of high spiritual quality and as a service, she kept covering the inside of the house. Before its purification, the inside of the Ka'bah was a place of refuge where people cooked, drank, and even went about unclothed.

There was a time when the number of people at the sanctuary became so great that expansion was necessary, but the people who lived in the area refused to give up their houses. No solution could be found to ease the overcrowded conditions. Finally, the problem was brought before one of the leaders of the Prophet's House, who told the Governor of Mecca to ask these people what claim they had to their houses. Their reply was that they owned their houses because their families had been there for centuries. Upon receiving their reply, this great man told the Governor to ask them if they were there before the House of Allah. The people replied that of course the House was there first. Upon hearing their reply he instructed the Governor to send back a message saying, 'The Owner of the House has a greater claim than you do, so give us room.' Space was made available, and the sanctuary was expanded.

The Station of Abraham (*Maqām Ibrāhīm*, مَقَام إِبْرَاهِيم) is a special spot near the Ka'bah. This is where the Prophet Abraham once stood when he and his son Ishmael were building the Ka'bah. The spot may have had a patch of mud, where he left a footprint which later turned to stone. The mark of his foot is still recognizable.

The Arabic word for pilgrimage (*ḥajj*, حَج) is related to many interesting words such as 'evidence, argument, proof' (*ḥujjah*, حُجَّة). One must give evidence of one's obedience and submission before embarking upon the Pilgrimage to Allah. Thus the pilgrim settles his affairs so that he is free from pressing worldly matters. The rites of Islam are purificatory: to become a pure person one must begin with oneself. On setting out on the Pilgrimage one should be cleansed and dedicated exclusively to the service of Allah, as though one will never come back again. Some people, in fact, never do return to their homes, either dying on the journey or staying on in Mecca or Medina.

The way is made easy for man once he makes himself available for worship, thus proving his submission and obedience. This is the key to everything on the spiritual path. If a person is not committed and sincere, progress can never take place.

قُلْ يَا أَهْلَ الْكِتَابِ لِمَ تَكْفُرُونَ بِآيَاتِ اللَّهِ
وَاللَّهُ شَهِيدٌ عَلَىٰ مَا تَعْمَلُونَ

98 **Say: O People of the Book, why do you disbelieve in the communications of Allah? And Allah is a witness of what you do.**

After seeing the evidence that Abraham was a prophet of Allah, neither a Jew nor a Christian, and that all those who came after him confirmed the one true message, why then do we still deny the signs of Allah? Allah is a witness for us and we are witnesses for ourselves.

قُلْ يَا أَهْلَ الْكِتَابِ لِمَ تَصُدُّونَ عَنْ سَبِيلِ اللَّهِ
مَنْ آمَنَ تَبْغُونَهَا عِوَجًا وَأَنْتُمْ شُهَدَاءُ وَمَا
اللَّهُ بِغَافِلٍ عَمَّا تَعْمَلُونَ

99 **Say: O People of the Book! Why do you hinder one who believes from the way of Allah? You seek to make the way crooked while you are witnesses, and Allah is not heedless of what you do.**

The Arabic word for 'to hinder' (*sadda*, سَدَّ) also means 'to block, prevent'. Why do the People of the Book stop others from following the right path? Why do they want people to turn away from the only way of Allah? The People of the Book try to make believers deviate by knowingly creating discord, differences and doubts and by mixing the true with the false. Why do they do that, if they profess to be people of the Book? The Book issues from one single Author, and His authorship is continued and perfected in the prophecy of Muhammad.

يَا أَيُّهَا الَّذِينَ آمَنُوا إِن تُطِيعُوا فَرِيقًا مِّنَ الَّذِينَ
أُوتُوا الْكِتَابَ يَرُدُّوكُم بَعْدَ
إِيمَانِكُمْ كَافِرِينَ

100 O you who believe! If you obey a party of those who have been given the Book, they will turn you back as non-believers after you have believed.

There were people with the Prophet who were afflicted by doubt and could easily be swayed, even though they had accepted Islam and taken refuge in Medina with the Prophet while the people of disbelief (*kufr*, كُفر) were still strong. This verse tells us that if we have seen the light of truth within ourselves, then it is incumbent upon us to believe that the All-Merciful Creator wants the best for us, and that we will come to know the meaning and purpose of creation under His Lordship. If we immerse ourselves in the culture of those who disbelieve, however, we will lose everything. Doubts and confusions are a test for us to strengthen our foundations: they are like the wind blowing upon a tree. The roots of faith must go deep if the tree is to remain standing. If we are too weak, doubts will break us and we will turn away from the truth, uprooted. This verse warns the Muslims not to trust those who have no faith in Allah.

وَكَيْفَ تَكْفُرُونَ وَأَنتُمْ تُتْلَىٰ عَلَيْكُمْ
آيَاتُ اللَّهِ وَفِيكُمْ رَسُولُهُ وَمَن يَعْتَصِم بِاللَّهِ
فَقَدْ هُدِيَ إِلَىٰ صِرَاطٍ مُّسْتَقِيمٍ

101 How can you disbelieve while it is you to whom the signs of Allah are recited, and among you is His Messenger? And whoever holds fast to Allah, he indeed is guided to the right path.

Allah continues to warn us: 'After you have seen the signs of Allah everywhere, how can you, the believer, knowingly wander into darkness and denial?' In this verse the signs of Allah are the Qur'an, the Prophet, the continuance of the message and the development of the way to Allah through the Prophet's community. Indeed, the self itself bears all the signs.

Man can find ultimate safety only by taking refuge in Allah, by clinging to a firm foundation, an inner refuge that can be relied upon totally. There is no refuge except with Allah.

يَا أَيُّهَا الَّذِينَ آمَنُوا اتَّقُوا اللَّهَ حَقَّ تُقَاتِهِ
وَلَا تَمُوتُنَّ إِلَّا وَأَنتُم مُّسْلِمُونَ

102 O you who believe, guard your duty to Allah with the care that is due to Him, and do not reach your death without being in submission.

Allah warns us of the negative attitudes that can cause us to deviate from the path. These include doubt, uncertainty, disagreement, and association with those who are not knowledgeable and firm in their faith, or with those who claim to be

People of the Book but who are not following the path of the real Book.

When Ja'far al-Ṣādiq was asked about this verse he said, 'You are truly careful of your duty to Allah if you obey Allah and His laws.' He also said, 'Do not talk about Allah, talk about the creation of Allah.' There are numerous traditions that enjoin us not to discuss the nature or essence of Allah, but rather to look at His Attributes and see the perfection of Allah's creation and His natural laws. By understanding these we will move closer to the knowledge of Allah. While intellect develops through reasoning and subtler cognition, the heart develops the intuitive dimension of the self. When the intellect can deal efficiently with the physical, natural world, and the heart with the Unseen, we as human beings can then deal with the gross and the subtle simultaneously.

To know Allah we start by obeying the outer laws. By keeping to the bounds and thereby preserving our energies, we then begin to understand the subtler laws. We must start by following the outward, divinely revealed Law (*Sharī'ah,* شَرِيعَة). This commitment brings about awareness and remembrance of the Creator, even when we transgress. In realizing our transgression, we are reminded of Allah. This remembrance leads us to greater awareness, until we reach the stage of true thankfulness: we are thankful for being given the opportunity to see the perfection of creation and for being given the opportunity to be in gratitude. When we are grateful, we are naturally motivated to follow the laws, and we do not want to be distracted. Gratitude is a symptom of unity (*tawḥīd,* تَوْحِيد). They are complementary: one leads to the other.

To achieve the state of gratitude, it may even be necessary to begin by pretending to be grateful, or at least, by professing gratefulness. Affirming one's Islam and one's unquestioned submission is, in a sense, a pretence at first. But continual remembrance of gratitude and contentment will eventually lead to actual and positive experience of Allah's mercy.

We must always give Allah His due and remember that we are not separate or disconnected from Him. Our 'I-ness' is only because of His 'He-ness'. We give Allah His due by accepting the divinely revealed laws. If we do not obey them, we subject ourselves to harm, distress, confusion and ultimately disaster, on personal and social levels. A vice such as usury may begin at an individual level, and eventually reach such proportions that, due to the overwhelming oppression of banks and related institutions, a whole culture could break down and vanish. Man must seek to create an environment in which the highest values predominate, values such as obedience, remembrance, gratitude, sharing and caring among all people.

'Alī said, 'One who is not grateful does not accept His Lordship.' A true seeker cannot be in a state other than gratitude, even though he may not like what faces him. He is gen inely, inwardly, freely grateful. Though a man may be confronted with injustice, he may take appropriate action and still be grateful for being given the opportunity either to correct the injustice or to escape if he cannot. Whoever is not grateful in all circumstances is lacking in knowledge.

'And do not die unless you are in submission.' What matters is the end. We must never depart from the path of action, but continue to strive for submission before we meet death. A Muslim is not in Islam unless he knows to whom he submits. We come to know Allah by recognizing His creation, His acts and His Attributes. We must be like Abraham, whom the Qur'an describes thus: 'He was an upright man, a Muslim.' He had complete trust, and sufficient knowledge to confirm to himself, both subjectively and objectively, that everything would be given to him as he needed it.

وَاعْتَصِمُوا بِحَبْلِ اللَّهِ جَمِيعًا وَلَا تَفَرَّقُوا ۚ وَاذْكُرُوا نِعْمَتَ
اللَّهِ عَلَيْكُمْ إِذْ كُنْتُمْ أَعْدَاءً فَأَلَّفَ بَيْنَ قُلُوبِكُمْ
فَأَصْبَحْتُمْ بِنِعْمَتِهِ إِخْوَانًا وَكُنْتُمْ عَلَىٰ شَفَا حُفْرَةٍ
مِنَ النَّارِ فَأَنْقَذَكُمْ مِنْهَا ۗ كَذَٰلِكَ يُبَيِّنُ اللَّهُ
لَكُمْ آيَاتِهِ لَعَلَّكُمْ تَهْتَدُونَ

103 And hold fast to the rope of Allah all together, and do not be divided. Remember the favour of Allah upon you when you were enemies, then He united your hearts; by His favour you became brethren. You were on the brink of a pit of fire, and He saved you from it. Thus does Allah make clear His signs that you may be guided.

The leaders of guidance among the Prophet's House were asked about the meaning of 'the rope of Allah' (*ḥabl Allāh*, حَبْل الله). A frequent answer was that it referred to the Qur'an and the Prophet. The rope of Allah is the line of safety which exists under all circumstances: it is wisdom and the enlightened intellect.

There was much tribal conflict, aggression and brutality in Arabia before the advent of the Prophetic message. Unfortunately, some pre-Islamic tribal characteristics can still be seen today. The Qur'an asks us to look at the blessedness of Islam because it is something which all people share. The values which it calls upon the Muslim to uphold are generosity, compassion and brotherhood. As a result of the Islamic code, even enemies become like brothers. A Muslim can travel the length or breadth of the earth and still find brotherhood in the house of another true Muslim, even if they share nothing of race, culture or language. This undeniable proof of the brotherhood of Islam has existed for 1400 years, and will increase in diversity and richness to the end of man's time on earth.

'You were on the brink of a pit of fire.' Because the people did not know how to conduct themselves, they were perilously near the Fire (of the Next Life), and it was only their fragile existence that separated them from it. Death could have taken them there immediately. The depth of this statement can be felt only by those who have been brought back from the edge of individual catastrophe into the mercy of Islam.

The Qur'an guides humankind towards the true life of Islam; the need for brotherhood, friendship and companionship is ingrained in man's innate disposition. There are many verses with this message. In the collection of 'Alī's speeches, letters and sayings ('The Pursuit of Eloquence', *Nahj al-Balāghah,* نَهج البَلاغة), he frequently talks of gathering and being together. 'The hand of Allah is with the gathering of people' (*yad Allāh ma'a al-jamā'ah,* يَد اللـه مَعَ الجَمَاعة) relates the well-known Prophetic saying. The people of Allah hold on to each other, work with each other, help each other, are brothers and sisters to each other, are close to one another, and avoid those who are not like them until they are strong enough not to be led astray.

The contents of Islam are humility, truthfulness and love for one another. But as Imam 'Alī once said when speaking about Islam and the future dispersion of Muslims: 'A day will come upon Islam when it will be thrown out just as one throws dishwater out of a pot.' The Muslim must be fearfully aware of his duty to Allah, for if he is not, he will end up an empty container.

وَلْتَكُن مِّنكُمْ أُمَّةٌ يَدْعُونَ إِلَى الْخَيْرِ وَيَأْمُرُونَ بِالْمَعْرُوفِ
وَيَنْهَوْنَ عَنِ الْمُنكَرِ ۚ وَأُولَٰئِكَ هُمُ الْمُفْلِحُونَ

104 **And let there be among you a community who call to good, enjoin what is right and forbid wrong. They shall be the successful ones.**

Enjoining good and forbidding evil is necessary for the existence of an Islamic community. There is something within all of us that naturally pushes us toward good. The source of this impulse is a higher consciousness, an urge that we often refer to as our conscience. Some of these values are specific to a particular culture, though most are timeless and are found in all cultures. What is genuinely good is always known to be so. The verbal root of 'good' (*ma'rūf,* مَعْرُوف) in this verse is 'to know' (*'arafa,* عَرَفَ) and a related noun means 'self-knowledge' (*'irfān,* عِرْفَان) or 'gnosis'. Every heart is constantly reminded of the desire to do good and to prohibit wrong. The root of 'wrong' (*munkar,* مُنْكَر) means 'to deny, to be ignorant of' (*nakira,* نَكِرَ): what is 'wrong' is something which is in and of itself denied.

'They shall be the successful ones.' The verbal root of 'success' (*falaḥ,* فَلاَح) means 'to turn, to change; to till, plough, split, cultivate' (*falaḥa,* فَلَحَ). One must be willing to turn the fertile soil of one's heart. Properly prepared and renewed, the heart can then sustain growth that will eventually prove fruitful.

وَلَا تَكُونُوا كَالَّذِينَ تَفَرَّقُوا وَاخْتَلَفُوا مِن بَعْدِ
مَا جَاءَهُمُ الْبَيِّنَاتُ ۚ وَأُولَٰئِكَ لَهُمْ عَذَابٌ عَظِيمٌ

105 **Do not be like those who became divided, and disagreed after clear proofs had come to them. They shall have a grievous chastisement.**

يَوْمَ تَبْيَضُّ وُجُوهٌ وَتَسْوَدُّ وُجُوهٌ ۚ فَأَمَّا الَّذِينَ اسْوَدَّتْ
وُجُوهُهُمْ أَكَفَرْتُمْ بَعْدَ إِيمَانِكُمْ فَذُوقُوا الْعَذَابَ
بِمَا كُنْتُمْ تَكْفُرُونَ

106 **On the day when [some] faces shall turn white and [some] faces shall turn black, then, those that turned black will be asked : Did you disbelieve after your belief? Taste, therefore, the chastisement, because you disbelieved.**

Those who disagree after clear proofs have been presented to them (and who therefore do not act upon them) will suffer grievously. Those who disagree about the imminent collapse of the biosphere's ecology are bound to suffer grievously. Those who disagree about, or justify the corruption of, the moral foundations of western civilization will suffer its final collapse. Those who disagree about the enslavement of the global population to an economic system controlled by an elite will suffer its final breakdown.

This verse describes the day when there will be no grey areas, when all will be made clear without justification or excuse, that is, on the Day of Reckoning. Whoever has lived a life of submission and love of Allah, and whoever has lived a life of selfish attachment to this world, will be made clear.

وَأَمَّا الَّذِينَ ابْيَضَّتْ وُجُوهُهُمْ فَفِي
رَحْمَةِ اللَّهِ هُمْ فِيهَا خَالِدُونَ

107 **And as for those whose faces shall turn white, they shall abide in Allah's mercy forever.**

With the affliction of this world now finished (after death), they find themselves forever in His mercy. That mercy can also be tasted now, and the purification of the 'face' can only be started in this life, for it is an active process. In the next life one will experience only the results of one's actions in this life. The whole story begins here and now, in this existence.

تِلْكَ آيَاتُ اللَّهِ نَتْلُوهَا عَلَيْكَ بِالْحَقِّ
وَمَا اللَّهُ يُرِيدُ ظُلْمًا لِّلْعَالَمِينَ

108 These are the signs of Allah which we recite to you with truth; and Allah does not desire any injustice to [His] creatures.

The signs of Allah are forever manifest before us. The reality of our situation reflects this, both inwardly and outwardly. What we really seek among this multiplicity is the knowledge of oneness; but human beings are weak, prone to the comfort of habit, and are enemies of what they do not know. Yet when we begin the path towards inner knowledge, this basic condition changes.

'And Allah does not desire any injustice to [His] creatures.' This refers to all systems, both known and unknown. Creation is based on balance and mercy; Allah has inscribed mercy upon Himself.

وَلِلَّهِ مَا فِي السَّمَاوَاتِ وَمَا فِي الْأَرْضِ
وَإِلَى اللَّهِ تُرْجَعُ الْأُمُورُ

109 Whatever is in the heavens and the earth belongs to Allah, and to Allah all things return.

Man must purify himself of inner vices and the rejection of

reality, or he will perish both individually and as a species. This is the meaning of fearing Allah as is His due. This is the reason for submission to His creational laws. One must first be in a state of awareness and gratitude for knowledge, then more knowledge and light will follow. Gratitude and contentment are signs of natural harmony. Being content is the beginning of growth, because in such a state one can absorb and assimilate more. To observe the forces at work within the creation, and yet consciously interact with them in a state of awareness, is to set in motion the process of obtaining self-knowledge and enlightenment.

كُنتُمْ خَيْرَ أُمَّةٍ أُخْرِجَتْ لِلنَّاسِ تَأْمُرُونَ بِالْمَعْرُوفِ
وَتَنْهَوْنَ عَنِ الْمُنكَرِ وَتُؤْمِنُونَ بِاللَّهِ وَلَوْ آمَنَ
أَهْلُ الْكِتَابِ لَكَانَ خَيْرًا لَّهُم مِّنْهُمُ الْمُؤْمِنُونَ
وَأَكْثَرُهُمُ الْفَاسِقُونَ

110 You are the best community brought forth among humankind. You enjoin what is right and forbid what is wrong and you believe in Allah. If the People of the Book had believed it would have been better for them; amongst them are believers, though most of them are transgressors.

The people who were closest to the Prophet obviously had the greatest opportunity to perfect themselves, because they were in the presence of the best example of humankind. They saw the birth of Islam in its final form and watched as it quickly evolved. Yet there were many who, despite the Prophet's presence, continued in their denial and hypocrisy.

'The best community' is the community of men and women which at any time best exemplifies the prophetic character, the character of true faith and trust in Allah.

True faith (*īmān*, إيمان) is believing in unity (*tawḥīd*, تَوْحيد), seeing nothing other than the one hand behind diverse forms, enjoining good deeds, and denying that which is to be denied, that is, falsehood. But the fulfilment of these conditions cannot be met without vigorous action. The laws of Allah are very clear and cannot be transgressed; we cannot simply speak about matters – good actions must match our words.

Islam was the completion and perfection of the messages brought by the previous prophets. All the books and the prophets taught submission, but the Qur'an was the last, complete book, and the Prophet Muhammad was the final messenger. The Muhammadan way perfected the path of submission. Among the People of the Book, specifically the Jews and Christians, are some who truly believe; but most of them are corrupt (*fāsiqūn*, فَاسِقُون) in their belief. They elevate their supposed spiritual source of guidance to an unreachable degree, so that they may justify their inability to fulfil what is required of them. Thus, Jesus becomes God and the Pope becomes his vicar, absolving people of their sins as long as they follow and support the church.

لَن يَضُرُّوكُمْ إِلَّآ أَذًى ۖ وَإِن يُقَٰتِلُوكُمْ
يُوَلُّوكُمُ ٱلْأَدْبَارَ ثُمَّ لَا يُنصَرُونَ

111 If they ever harm you it will be but a slight injury, and if they fight with you they shall turn [their] backs in flight; then shall they not be helped.

The harm inflicted upon the believer is very superficial because the non-believers have no conviction. They cling helplessly to this life, because they do not believe in the Hereafter. If the non-believers fight them, then the believers should know that they will not stand their ground; for they want this life and will run away for fear of death. The people of disbelief do not understand the state of a man of true faith. He is not, as they suppose, fatalistically suicidal. He is a person who genuinely believes that the purpose of this life is to prepare for the next, and if this opportunity for preparation is not allowed him and his community, he is willing to give up his life in an effort to attain it. He is not a terrorist. Those who commit acts of terrorism are not in Islam, though they may have been born Muslims. The Muslim respects life and accepts the importance of life, provided it can be lived in a state of worship.

ضُرِبَتْ عَلَيْهِمُ الذِّلَّةُ أَيْنَ مَا ثُقِفُوٓا إِلَّا بِحَبْلٍ
مِّنَ اللَّهِ وَحَبْلٍ مِّنَ النَّاسِ وَبَآءُو بِغَضَبٍ
مِّنَ اللَّهِ وَضُرِبَتْ عَلَيْهِمُ الْمَسْكَنَةُ ذَٰلِكَ بِأَنَّهُمْ كَانُوا
يَكْفُرُونَ بِآيَاتِ اللَّهِ وَيَقْتُلُونَ الْأَنبِيَآءَ بِغَيْرِ حَقٍّ
ذَٰلِكَ بِمَا عَصَوا وَّكَانُوا يَعْتَدُونَ

112 **Abasement has overcome them wherever they are found, except under a covenant with Allah and a covenant with men. They bring about Allah's wrath and incur their own humiliation, because they disbelieved in the signs of Allah and killed the prophets unjustly. Their disobedience exceeded the limits.**

Abasement (*dhillah*, ذِلَّة) overcomes anyone who is not in harmony with the will of Reality, because he does not recognize that everything comes from the One Reality. This verse also refers to the Jews who believed that they were the chosen élite and that their code of behaviour was superior to all others, a belief which led them to regard and treat other people as inferior. Their self-elevation will therefore be met by abasement, unless their existence is extended by life-support systems from Allah and man. Allah's life-support system is for everybody: the generosity He extends through nature is truly all-encompassing. But even the great generosity of nature which embraces everyone has a point beyond which it collapses.

The humiliation of abasement has struck the people who are bereft (*masākīn*, مَسَاكِين) and who have no access to that great opening which leads to the knowledge of Reality, because they have denied the science that Reality offers. How many prophets were killed by people who denied the truth? How many messengers were killed by arrogance? It is a clear sign of Allah's mercy and generosity that He has repeatedly sent these prophets and messengers to rejuvenate the teaching of truth, but people do not understand.

Whoever denies Allah and lives in arrogance is bereft, though be he a multi-millionaire outwardly. A wealthy person is often to be pitied more than one who is indigent. If the wealthy man has invested all his life's energy in acquiring material goods which, rather than being the source of joy he had expected them to be, turn out to be a source of worry and sorrow, clearly he is bereft. He sees that those around him care only for his money and not for him.

لَيْسُوا سَوَآءً مِّنْ أَهْلِ الْكِتَابِ أُمَّةٌ قَآئِمَةٌ يَتْلُونَ
ءَايَاتِ اللهِ ءَانَآءَ الَّيْلِ وَهُمْ يَسْجُدُونَ

113 They are not all alike. Among the People of the Book there is an upright community; they recite Allah's verses in the night, and they prostrate in adoration.

All the people of the Book are not the same. Amongst the Christians and the Jews are those who believe in Allah, but the majority do not.

يُؤْمِنُونَ بِاللَّهِ وَالْيَوْمِ الْآخِرِ وَيَأْمُرُونَ بِالْمَعْرُوفِ وَيَنْهَوْنَ
عَنِ الْمُنكَرِ وَيُسَارِعُونَ فِي الْخَيْرَاتِ ۖ
وَأُولَٰئِكَ مِنَ الصَّالِحِينَ

114 They believe in Allah and the Last Day, enjoin what is right and forbid the wrong, and hasten toward good deeds. They are among the righteous.

Allah defines the righteous among the People of the Book as those who have faith (*īmān*, إيمان) and are aware of the Oneness of Allah. They believe that the purpose of creation is to come to know Allah. Their actions are firm: they know what is right, and act upon what they know without compromising with falsehood.

The People of the Book who are exceptional rush forward to perform good deeds, since they possess the ability to render things well (*iṣlāḥ*, إصلاح). Two words are commonly used in Arabic for moving quickly towards something: the first word (*sur'ah*, سُرْعَة) is used in the context of hastening towards what is positive and this is the word used for 'hasten' in this verse. The other (*'ajalah*, عَجَلَة) implies hurrying towards something which has no connotation of benefit, for example: 'Were He to punish them for what they earn, He would certainly hasten the chastisement for them' (18: 58). The Qur'an is the book which distinguishes between opposites and setting limits. Without such discrimination, creation could not be sustained.

وَمَا يَفْعَلُوا مِنْ خَيْرٍ فَلَن يُكْفَرُوهُ ۗ
وَاللَّهُ عَلِيمٌ بِالْمُتَّقِينَ

115 And whatever good they do, they shall not be

denied it; and Allah knows those who cautiously guard themselves.

Every action has an equal and opposite reaction; the reverberation of any worthwhile action will resound in oneself. Allah knows who is aware, who is cautious, who is in the path and who is not. From the Qur'an and our traditions we are told that though we may not see Him, He always sees us.

إِنَّ الَّذِينَ كَفَرُوا لَن تُغْنِيَ عَنْهُمْ أَمْوَالُهُمْ وَلَا أَوْلَادُهُم
مِّنَ اللَّهِ شَيْئًا ۖ وَأُولَٰئِكَ أَصْحَابُ النَّارِ ۚ هُمْ فِيهَا خَالِدُونَ

116 Neither wealth nor children shall avail those who disbelieve against Allah; they are inmates of the fire wherein they shall abide forever.

Allah has repeatedly described man's weakness and hypocrisy, which are established by his past habits and social influences.

Those who deny the One Reality, the mercy of Allah, the blessedness of His love for His creation, and who deny the fact that man has come to this life in order to learn how to live well, how to bring up future generations well, and how to conduct himself in preparation for the next life, will not be helped in offsetting the justice of Allah by means of their wealth or offspring, or through any imagined source of power. All those things they depend upon in this transient world may give them a feeling of immediate security, but will ultimately lead to an affliction that is most certainly not transient. In the next life, people who have squandered their physical existence will be left in a state of eternal distraction.

مَثَلُ مَا يُنفِقُونَ فِي هَٰذِهِ الْحَيَوٰةِ الدُّنْيَا كَمَثَلِ
رِيحٍ فِيهَا صِرٌّ أَصَابَتْ حَرْثَ قَوْمٍ ظَلَمُوٓا أَنفُسَهُمْ
فَأَهْلَكَتْهُ ۚ وَمَا ظَلَمَهُمُ اللَّهُ وَلَٰكِنْ أَنفُسَهُمْ يَظْلِمُونَ

117 An analogy of what they spend in the life of this world is that of an intensely cold wind which smites and destroys the farmland of a people who have done themselves injustice. Allah is not unjust to them, but they are unjust to themselves.

This verse does not say that those who deny Reality have achieved nothing; on the contrary, they have built great empires and civilizations. The Qur'an describes the powerful and forceful societies they built and continue to build because it is energy that makes such things materialize. This energy is like a strong gale that carries with it the seeds of destruction. The destruction may come about spontaneously, or it may occur slowly, in a cyclical fashion.

No man has been born who will not die, and a man can be put to death well before his anticipated time. Thus, the energies and objectives of those in denial and distraction are here described like a wind which freezes the ploughed land. The power of actions which do not emanate from the path decreed by Allah can only be destructive.

Those who disbelieve try frantically to build for the future, but all will be destroyed because of their ignorance, lack of discrimination and injustice. The deeds of people or of societies which do not adhere to the decree of Allah will come to naught, not because Allah is unjust, but because they have brought injustice upon themselves. Knowledge is necessary in order for justice and discrimination to be applied. We are witnessing in our own age a great example of the injustice man can and does perpetrate upon himself: our most gracious and hospitable host, the planet earth, is being savagely looted without regard for the delicate balance of the eco-systems which replenish her. Her reaction to this callousness will become angrier as man's injustice increases. The strands are unravelling and snapping one by one as the weight of iniquity threatens to pull the human foundations of civilization into the yawning chasm of dissolution.

يَا أَيُّهَا الَّذِينَ آمَنُوا لَا تَتَّخِذُوا بِطَانَةً مِنْ دُونِكُمْ
لَا يَأْلُونَكُمْ خَبَالًا وَدُّوا مَا عَنِتُّمْ قَدْ بَدَتِ الْبَغْضَاءُ
مِنْ أَفْوَاهِهِمْ وَمَا تُخْفِي صُدُورُهُمْ أَكْبَرُ قَدْ بَيَّنَّا
لَكُمُ الْآيَاتِ إِنْ كُنْتُمْ تَعْقِلُونَ

118 **O you who believe, do not take for intimate friends other than your own people. They will cause confusion for you; they love the things that cause you hardship. Hatred has already appeared from their mouths, and what their hearts conceal is greater still. Indeed, We have made the signs clear for you, if you will but understand.**

Those who possess faith cannot become intimate with those who have none. This does not mean that the people of Allah should form exclusive clubs or mutual admiration societies: the injunction is meant as a protection. The Prophet said in a well-known tradition, 'If you are with a people for forty days you will become like them.' Man naturally connects to the familiar.

'They will cause you confusion.' Confusion (*khibāl*, خبال) implies distraction and chaos, a lack of consistency and guiding reason. Those people who are antagonistic to Islam cannot be taken as friends, for they support a system of beliefs and values that are not only not the same, but are even opposite. Though some are outwardly similar, the underlying intention is not towards Allah. These people are divided even among themselves and, as with any conflicting group, each eventually wants the other's demise and is pleased when it comes about. This is a natural animal, or lower, human tendency.

'And what their hearts conceal is greater still.' In other words, what appears is only the tip of the iceberg. These signs are clear. At the time this verse was revealed, it was the second or third year after the emigration (*hijrah*, هِجْرَة) to Medina, and Islam was gaining strength. The enemies of Islam were becoming inreasingly alarmed and some of them, especially those in Medina, were forced by circumstance to appear as followers of the Prophet, although they really harboured enmity toward him.

هَٰٓأَنتُمْ أُوْلَآءِ تُحِبُّونَهُمْ وَلَا يُحِبُّونَكُمْ وَتُؤْمِنُونَ
بِٱلْكِتَٰبِ كُلِّهِۦ وَإِذَا لَقُوكُمْ قَالُوٓا۟ ءَامَنَّا
وَإِذَا خَلَوْا۟ عَضُّوا۟ عَلَيْكُمُ ٱلْأَنَامِلَ مِنَ
ٱلْغَيْظِ ۚ قُلْ مُوتُوا۟ بِغَيْظِكُمْ ۗ إِنَّ ٱللَّهَ عَلِيمٌۢ بِذَاتِ ٱلصُّدُورِ

119 You would show them love while they do not love you, and you believe in the Book, all of it. When they meet you they say: We believe; but when they are alone, they bite [their] fingernails in rage against you. Say: Perish in your rage. Surely, Allah knows what is in the hearts.

This is a continuing description of the attitude of appeasement and hypocrisy displayed by the enemies of Islam as they observed the growth of this new religion. Allah addresses the believers, whose tendency is to love all humanity, all of Allah's creation. They may forget that creation in its human aspect has a choice of being either productive or counter-productive. A man whose real station is lower than an animal because of his aggressive disruptiveness can do nothing until, with the dawning of knowledge, he decides to change. Because of his love, the believer knows that man can change – 'He brings forth the living from the dead and He brings forth the dead from the living' (6: 95). Nothing is impossible. Our greatest enemy could suddenly become our best friend if only he were illuminated by the light of knowledge. It is also equally possible that the heart of our friend in faith could suddenly turn from the truth, and thus we might become the worst of enemies. These events occur all the time, and therefore we must regard even these relationships as transient.

This verse describes the quality of love that people of faith have as part of Allah's mercy (*raḥmah*, رَحْمَة), even though the object of affection may not reciprocate. Those who do not reciprocate, according to this verse, are hypocrites who seek only to appease. They secretly gnaw their fingernails in rage at the goodness of those who believe, this is done because they are afraid to express their anger directly.

إِن تَمْسَسْكُمْ حَسَنَةٌ تَسُؤْهُمْ وَإِن تُصِبْكُمْ سَيِّئَةٌ
يَفْرَحُوا بِهَا وَإِن تَصْبِرُوا وَتَتَّقُوا لَا يَضُرُّكُمْ كَيْدُهُمْ شَيْئًا
إِنَّ اللَّهَ بِمَا يَعْمَلُونَ مُحِيطٌ

120 If good befalls you, it grieves them, and if evil afflicts you, they are joyous. If you are patient and guard yourselves, their scheme will not injure you in the least. Surely, Allah encompasses and thoroughly comprehends what they do.

This is a continuation of the previous verse, describing the non-believers' duplicity and bad intentions. Allah says they dislike it whenever something good comes to the believers, while if any harm befalls the latter they celebrate. Whatever man considers acceptable, he desires to see increase; he does not like to be threatened by what he finds unacceptable to his own system of values. They are in reality already within the scheme of Allah, and He knows what they are really doing. It is our duty to carry on with our tasks and to obey Allah, being firm, correct, courageous, patient and cautious. We must seek redress for our grievances without holding anger against those who have wronged us. Our anger can be directed only against their ignorance and actions, not against them, for the nature of Allah's justice means we must hold nothing against any creature. We cannot hate another man, for though he is only as good as his actions, his actions may change tomorrow.

وَإِذْ غَدَوْتَ مِنْ أَهْلِكَ تُبَوِّئُ الْمُؤْمِنِينَ مَقَاعِدَ
لِلْقِتَالِ ۗ وَاللَّهُ سَمِيعٌ عَلِيمٌ

121 When you went forth early in the morning from your family to lodge the believers in encampments of war, and Allah is Hearing, Knowing.

إِذْ هَمَّتْ طَائِفَتَانِ مِنْكُمْ أَنْ تَفْشَلَا وَاللَّهُ وَلِيُّهُمَا ۗ
وَعَلَى اللَّهِ فَلْيَتَوَكَّلِ الْمُؤْمِنُونَ

122 And when two parties among you showed cowardice – Allah was the guardian of them both. And in Allah should the believers trust.

This verse refers to the time in Medina when the Prophet came out to decide on the Muslim battle positions against the enemy about to invade the town. It is related that while taking counsel on whether to fight from within the town or to meet the enemy outside, many people voiced the opinion that it was cowardly to remain within the city to fight; thus it was decided to meet the enemy on the outskirts of the city.

When the Prophet went out to the battlefield to plan his strategy for the battle, he took one clan each from the tribes of Aws and Khazraj, the two tribes who had originally invited the Prophet to Medina. The two clans were the Banu Salimah and the Banu Harithah, known as the 'two parties' (*ṭā'ifatān*, طَائِفَتَان), and the Prophet placed one on each flank of the Muslim line of defence. Before and during the battle the Muslims were weakened by a well-known hypocrite named 'Abdullah ibn Ubayy, a man prone to scheming and intrigue. He encouraged the Prophet's companions to follow the weaker tendencies within themselves. Hypocrisy (*nifāq*, نِفَاق) and weakness of faith was manifest so often among the Prophet's companions that 'Abbās ibn 'Abd al-Muṭṭalib is related to have said, 'So many verses were revealed about the hypocrites that we did not think any of the companions would be spared.' Hypocrisy was not rare, for its seeds already exist in every heart. When nourished it takes hold and spreads like wildfire. Hypocrisy is automatically strengthened when faith is depleted; similarly, if certainty is not nourished, doubt will increase. There is no point of neutrality. We inadvertently nourish the weeds of hypocrisy if we do not tend to the plants of faith in the garden of our heart. These plants are those higher qualities in us which need regular pruning and attention. Overnight, through inattention, the entire garden of the heart can be overrun with these choking weeds, and suddenly we find ourselves completely engulfed in hypocrisy.

Hypocrisy had made such headway among the Companions that they were about to lose their moral strength, yet while they followed His path and defended themselves Allah was their guardian and friend.

After the non-believers failed at Badr, having been beaten by a handful of Muslims, they carried their seventy dead back to Mecca and immediately began to plan a major offensive against the Muslims. They had considered Islam an insignificant force, and this arrogance caused their downfall at Badr. There is a saying that the smallest stone, when not given due respect, can crack one's skull: this is how divine justice eventually prevails.

وَلَقَدْ نَصَرَكُمُ ٱللَّهُ بِبَدْرٍ وَأَنتُمْ أَذِلَّةٌ فَٱتَّقُوا

ٱللَّهَ لَعَلَّكُمْ تَشْكُرُونَ

123 And certainly Allah assisted you at Badr when you were weak. So be careful of your duty to Allah that you may give thanks.

In anyone's life there are occasions when Allah's mercy is at first not evidently manifest; later, however, it becomes clear, as one is fulfilled in a particular situation. Allah reminds us of this phenomenon by mentioning the Battle of Badr. 'You were weak (*adhillah*, أَذِلَّة) and Allah gave you victory.' Allah gave the Muslims victory at Badr through the strength of their trust and brotherhood. They knew they had to defend themselves and work together because they were few in number. In the case of Uḥud, however, the Muslims became arrogant, and through their arrogance *Shayṭan* entered their weakened hearts.

Muslims are asked to remember Badr in this verse; to remember how weak they were, yet gloriously victorious by their unity and obedience to the Prophet. Though they were a small band, underfed, under–dressed, under-equipped and outnumbered, victory came by Allah's command just as the loss at Uhud was by Allah's command. At Badr they were the hand of Allah, but at Uḥud they were the hand of hypocrisy. Allah cautions them, therefore, to be wary of Him and to guard against their ignorance.

Naturally, no one is grateful for failure *per se*; however one should be grateful for attaining the knowledge of the perfect laws that govern existence. Furthermore, one should be grateful that Allah's laws do not change: 'You will find no change in the way of Allah' (33: 62).

Traditions relate that the number of men Abu Sufyān led against the Muslims at the Battle of Uḥud was 3,000, more than half of them mounted. They were well equipped with 200 archers and the chief lieutenant of Abu Sufyān was Khālid ibn al-Walād.

At the beginning of the battle the forces of Islam, which numbered about 700, first held their ground and later overpowered the enemy. They then began to loot. There is nothing inherently wrong in taking the spoils of battle, but the Prophet reminded them not to occupy themselves with this until victory was certain. When the group of fifty archers, led by Abdullah ibn Jubayr, who were protecting the Muslims' flank saw the other Muslims looting, they complained to him that they would not get any of the spoils if they did not go at once to claim their share. Then, in spite of the reminder from Abdullah that the Prophet had given firm orders for them not to move from their positions, they ran off to take their share of the booty. The battle immediately turned against the Muslims. At this point the Prophet suffered a great many wounds, so many that he fell to the ground, and it was rumoured that he was dead. He was left with only two men defending him, 'Alī and one other Companion: everyone else had fled. 'Alī's sword broke after he had killed nine of the enemy in succession. The Prophet, bleeding from dozens of wounds, gave 'Alī his sword.

إِذْ تَقُولُ لِلْمُؤْمِنِينَ أَلَن يَكْفِيَكُمْ أَن يُمِدَّكُمْ
رَبُّكُم بِثَلَٰثَةِ ءَالَٰفٍ مِّنَ ٱلْمَلَٰٓئِكَةِ مُنزَلِينَ

124 Then you said to the believers: Does it not suffice

you that your Lord would assist you by sending three thousand angels?

بَلَىٰٓ ۚ إِن تَصْبِرُوا۟ وَتَتَّقُوا۟ وَيَأْتُوكُم مِّن فَوْرِهِمْ هَـٰذَا يُمْدِدْكُمْ رَبُّكُم
بِخَمْسَةِ ءَالَـٰفٍ مِّنَ ٱلْمَلَـٰٓئِكَةِ مُسَوِّمِينَ

125 **Surely, if you remain patient and cautiously guard yourselves, even if they come upon you in a headlong manner, your Lord will assist you with five thousand forceful angels.**

وَمَا جَعَلَهُ ٱللَّهُ إِلَّا بُشْرَىٰ لَكُمْ وَلِتَطْمَئِنَّ قُلُوبُكُم بِهِۦ
وَمَا ٱلنَّصْرُ إِلَّا مِنْ عِندِ ٱللَّهِ ٱلْعَزِيزِ ٱلْحَكِيمِ

126 **And Allah gave you the good news so that your hearts might be at ease. Help and victory are only from Allah, the Mighty, the Wise.**

After the battle it was clear that the Muslim forces had been soundly defeated because of their arrogance; most had scattered and run away. Such was the state of Islam in the third year after the emigration, after sixteen years of prophethood. The loss at Uḥud continues to be a lesson for us, against the divisiveness that occurs and quickly usurps man's self-control when his lower tendencies dominate.

Had it not been for the intervention of Allah's divine will which rectified the situation, they would have been completely destroyed, and Islam would have come to an end. At the Battle of Badr the angelic powers had been made manifest to help restore the hearts of the weak and to weaken the hearts of the enemy: and it seemed to the enemy that the Muslims were more than double their actual number because of the energy the Muslims exhibited, their dynamism and their unity. When hearts are completely united, one plus one does not equal two, but much more than that; but once a little tarnish appears upon those hearts, however, the formula changes: then it is not even as much as two. It was through Allah that the Muslims came out of the Battle of Uḥūd without being totally destroyed.

The man of true faith will also be saved, even though he may appear to have lost, because Allah will never lose, and Allah's way will always prevail. One who has completely abandoned himself to that way will inevitably be saved. This victory, however, does not always come about because of his own efforts. They may, in fact, cause failure, as in the case of Uḥūd. The Muslims' collective efforts resulted in failure, because they gave in to their lower tendencies and were thus unable to remain unified.

لِيَقْطَعَ طَرَفًا مِّنَ الَّذِينَ كَفَرُوٓا
أَوْ يَكْبِتَهُمْ فَيَنقَلِبُوا خَآئِبِينَ

127 That He may cut off a portion of those who disbelieve, or suppress them so that they would return unsuccessful and disappointed.

The root of 'to suppress' means to crush, restrain or subdue (*kabata,* كَبَتَ). In colloquial Arabic the word means suppression of some emotion, such as anger. In classical Arabic it refers to the suppression due to shame and loss. The implication is that to keep anything to oneself indicates a lack of courage. From the viewpoint of Arab culture, suppressing oneself means having no self-esteem.

In seeking to understand the Qur'an we see how important it is to delve deeply into the Arabic language, for the Qur'an cannot simply be translated. One word may have two or three different meanings, although one meaning can be the most appropriate within the context of the sentence. The other meanings, however, still contribute to the deeper meaning of the word. An example of this which goes along with the idea of suppression is its opposite, which is expression. The root verb which means 'to express' is the very same to which the name 'Arab' is connected. Someone who could not express himself was not considered a man, was not in unity with his being. Thus, to speak so boldly of suppression among the Arabs was seriously to offend their race.

لَيْسَ لَكَ مِنَ ٱلْأَمْرِ شَيْءٌ أَوْ يَتُوبَ عَلَيْهِمْ
أَوْ يُعَذِّبَهُمْ فَإِنَّهُمْ ظَالِمُونَ

128 You have no obligation in the affair whether He turns to them mercifully or chastises them, for surely they are unjust.

Allah is telling the Prophet that this battle, or any matter, was not his concern but Allah's. He explains that what occurred was part of His creation, His kingdom, and His arena of action. The Prophet's only option was to be a true slave of Allah. He was not to concern himself with gain or loss in this battle or any other action: results belong to Allah.

Allah may forgive some people, or afflict them more for their injustices. Elsewhere in the Qur'an it says, 'And We did not do them injustice, but they were unjust to themselves' (11: 101).

The Prophet is commanded to continue to deliver His message and uphold His way, whether it is accepted or not. When the 700 or so Muslims suddenly disappeared and he was left with only a few men, the Prophet said, 'There is no courageous young man like 'Alī and no sword but *Dhu al-fiqār* (ذُو الفِقار), the name of the sword of 'Alī.' The Prophet had no other recourse but to call upon Allah.

Allah tells the Prophet that he is merely a messenger and can do only his best. He knows the path and the truth, and yet he must leave the rest to Allah, because the outcome is not in his hands: 'Your Lord knows best about you. If He wills He will grant you mercy and if He wills He will punish you. We have not sent you [Muhammad] to them as a guardian' (17: 54). He is reminded that should others exalt him because he had miraculously survived the battle, his salvation was not of his own doing. 'Nothing is incumbent upon the Messenger but delivery of the message' (5: 99).

وَلِلَّهِ مَا فِي السَّمَاوَاتِ وَمَا فِي الْأَرْضِ يَغْفِرُ لِمَن يَشَاءُ
وَيُعَذِّبُ مَن يَشَاءُ وَاللَّهُ غَفُورٌ رَّحِيمٌ

129 Whatever is in the heavens and the earth belongs to Allah. He forgives whom He will and chastises whom He will. And Allah is Forgiving, Merciful.

All that is in the heavens and earth belongs to Allah and is under His command and power. Within that power, man has been given relative freedom to act. If he acts correctly, then his action will be successful, because it will be in harmony with the natural laws and Allah's decree; but if he does not, then he will have to learn by suffering to revise his actions. It is to be hoped that he will learn before it is too late.

'And Allah is Forgiving, Merciful.' The forgiveness and mercy of Allah are operative at all times, even though man may find himself at a loss. Agony, chastisement, and affliction are part of His mercy. If man does not see His mercy in every situation, then he has superimposed his own values, attachments and desires on Allah's continuous mercy. Because of these ever-flowing gifts of forgiveness and mercy, the person of faith cannot but be sufficiently thankful. One who does not show gratitude and praise is weak in faith and understanding.

يَٰٓأَيُّهَا ٱلَّذِينَ ءَامَنُوا۟ لَا تَأْكُلُوا۟ ٱلرِّبَوٰٓا۟ أَضْعَٰفًا
مُّضَٰعَفَةً ۖ وَٱتَّقُوا۟ ٱللَّهَ لَعَلَّكُمْ تُفْلِحُونَ

130 O you who believe, do not devour usury, multiplying it over and over. Be careful of your duty to Allah, that you may be successful.

The Qur'an consistently and effortlessly moves across time and space, dealing with the heavens and earth, time and timelessness, this life and the next, the fire in this life and that in the next, in order that we may taste the vastness of the unity of creational reality. Thus, the Qur'an moves from a verse concerning the cosmos to one concerning domestic or existential matters such as wives and children, moving in the next verse to something else again. The Qur'an is the guide to the One Reality manifested in the realm of duality, the essence of which is one; Allah be praised.

In order that a community may be united within a socially responsible system, usury, whether on a small or large scale, is forbidden. The Qur'an warns us not to 'devour usury', no matter how it is calculated. Interest (*ribā*, ربا) implies abuse, and exploitation is involved in lending and borrowing money with conditions. The verbal root of usury means 'to increase, to grow, to exceed, to be more than'. The implication is that of an unnatural increase in scale and thereby a disturbance in the balance. Someone who extracts interest is severing the connection to balanced life and the higher qualities of humanity. When a person in need of money is expected to pay back more than he has borrowed, he finds himself oppressed by the system or person that has extended the loan. Since he did not have the essential funds to begin with, it would be even more stressful to demand that he return more than what he essentially needed.

Much of the banking system is based on 'legalized' exploitation and usury, though it may not be classified as usury in the narrowest sense, because banks never lend money to those who are truly in need and who do not have collateral. They loan to those from whom they are most certain to recover the entire sum loaned plus interest payments. This system creates a situation in which there are many people who are desperately seeking a means to repay their debts. Banks want to participate in business or trade without the natural consequence of business risk. They want to establish a guaranteed return irrespective of the outcome of the venture. This guarantee is not allowed in Islam, for it is unnatural and out of balance. Furthermore, interest loans are usually given on the basis of financial projections which show a continuous increase in profit. This is highly unnatural, because businesses and economies fluctuate. Because of this unnatural expectation for continuous increase, financial empires begin to tremble at the mere mention of earnings being lower than expected for a particular quarter. Any government, business, or individual dependent on large amounts of debt for its operations exists on the most tenuous of foundations.

The world banking system, by the use of interest loans and other financial controls which allow banks to create money, holds governments and their people in its vice-like grip. This system is calculated, from every angle, not to absorb the natural risk of financial ventures. For example, in the United States, if a debtor defaults on a loan, it is the American people themselves who have to make good the loan. The American taxpayers, even though they had no involvement whatsoever with the failed business investment or attached government subsidies, end up repaying the debt. The system of debt that is firmly entrenched throughout the world financial community is a malignancy that has enslaved its people. It is at the source of monetary inflation and incalculably large government deficits that threaten the ruin of the mightiest nations. The system of debt that exists today has subjugated Third World countries so that the people of these countries remain bound in utter poverty and destitution. Western governments support puppet leaders in these countries who sell their resources to western businesses and borrow money from western banks for modern technological developments that do not in any way enhance the lives of the common people, who do not even have roads to get their meagre farm produce to market. For this reason, the Qur'an speaks so strongly against the system of usury: 'Those who devour interest will not rise except like one who has joined hands with Shayṭān. They say: But interest loans are like conducting normal business! Rather, Allah permits normal buying and selling but forbids the use of interest ... Allah will destroy usury and He will cause charitable deeds to prosper ... And if you do not desist, take note that war will be waged by Allah and His Messenger' (2: 275-279).

The ideal Islamic lending situation works through returns on loans that come about as a result of profit-sharing. The bank's funds are used as business investments, and are not invested with conditional returns in the form of one-sided interest rates. If the business venture does well, then the bank does well; if not, it fares according to the results of the business.

Allah warns us to guard our transactions and to realize that by supporting usury we are introducing an unnatural, oppressive system that cannot sustain itself. Ultimately, this system will push beyond its tolerance limit and collapse, and then disruption of life will occur.

وَاتَّقُوا النَّارَ الَّتِي أُعِدَّتْ لِلْكَافِرِينَ

131 And carefully guard yourselves against the Fire which has been prepared for the non-believers.

The 'fire' of this world is the constant agitation of disharmony, disruption and war. We must be conscious of the great opportunity we have been given to perfect our worship by understanding the unity of the source of all creation. Worship without knowledge is of limited use; prayer without knowledge of Allah has little value. The Prophet said, 'The reflection of one hour is better than seventy years of worship.' The Prophet also said, 'The sleep of a man of knowledge is better than the worship of a man of ignorance.' The teaching contained within the Qur'an is concerned with self-knowledge and knowledge of the Lord of creation.

The opportunity to reflect is of crucial importance. Observation shows that most people, even those who are outwardly successful, are preoccupied with the existential struggle and constant effort to make ends meet. Their lives are beset with stress, and uncertainty of any real fulfilment. This inner void is the affliction for those who have no faith and do not exert themselves to enhance their inner spiritual resources.

وَأَطِيعُوا اللَّهَ وَالرَّسُولَ لَعَلَّكُمْ تُرْحَمُونَ

132 And obey Allah and the Messenger that you may be shown mercy.

Clearly, one who wishes to follow the path of knowledge must obey Allah and His prophets, but one cannot be certain of following the Prophet of Allah unless one also follows those of whom the Prophet would approve. The Prophet clearly and repeatedly pointed out those from whom the Muslims were to take their guidance. But the Muslims who came after broke up into diverse groups and clans. They concerned themselves more with the establishing of worldly kingdoms and a religion that could be approved of by worldly rulers. Some Muslims even dared to claim that many followers would leave Islam if the strict laws of the Prophet were insisted upon, and therefore favoured slackening the boundaries of guidance to gain more adherents.

There is no clear way for humankind other than the Muhammadan way, and the leaders on this path cannot be found through popular elections. This leadership is transmitted through revolution – the revolution or turning of the purified heart – and virtuous actions. The Prophet's heir cannot possibly be chosen by popular vote, because this manner of election is dominated by the lower values. Real leaders, like Islam itself, cannot be forced upon people. They have to be chosen and then followed.

وَسَارِعُوٓا۟ إِلَىٰ مَغْفِرَةٍ مِّن رَّبِّكُمْ وَجَنَّةٍ عَرْضُهَا
السَّمٰوٰتُ وَالْأَرْضُ أُعِدَّتْ لِلْمُتَّقِينَ

133 Hasten to forgiveness from your Lord and a Garden as expansive as the heavens and the earth, prepared for those who guard themselves cautiously.

To hasten to a good cause is to rush towards forgiveness from the Lord. The Lord is He Who brings one to the knowledge that everything seen and experienced issues from Him. If one rushes towards that recognition, one will soon see nothing other than the 'Garden as expansive as the heavens and the earth'. The phrase implies that the Garden encompasses everything. Allah's mercy, like the Garden, encompasses even what appears as affliction. Once the cause of affliction is recognized, contentment descends upon the heart. Contentment is an example of the state experienced in the Garden.

When this verse was revealed, the Prophet was asked this question: 'If the Garden is as wide as the heavens and the earth, then where is the Fire?' He answered by saying, 'Where is the night when day comes?' This implies that the turmoil and trouble of the Fire are hidden within, and the fire-extinguisher is contentment, which then becomes a door to the Garden. Contentment is found in faith and correct action: to be content is to experience inner expansion and ease. To be discontent is to experience inner tightness and constriction.

The mercy (*raḥmah*, رَحْمَة) of Allah encompasses everything for those who guard themselves. Once, when the Prophet was seen smiling to himself, he was asked for the reason for his pleasure. He said, 'No difficulty can win over two eases.' He was referring to the verse of the Qur'an: 'Surely with difficulty is ease, with difficulty is ease' (94:-5-6). Every difficulty will pass; if not during one's lifetime, ease will at least come with death. When we see how our difficulties come about, we see the perfect and intricate way that cause and effect come together. This knowledge provides another ease and comfort. Thus, we have double ease with each difficulty.

ٱلَّذِينَ يُنفِقُونَ فِى ٱلسَّرَّآءِ وَٱلضَّرَّآءِ وَٱلْكَـٰظِمِينَ ٱلْغَيْظَ
وَٱلْعَافِينَ عَنِ ٱلنَّاسِ ۗ وَٱللَّهُ يُحِبُّ ٱلْمُحْسِنِينَ

134 Those who spend in ease as well as in adversity; those who restrain [their] anger and pardon men, and Allah loves those who do good.

For those who are free, both difficulty and ease are acceptable. They spend their energy and their wealth; they do not hold on to things. Their time, their wealth, their lives are given in the way of Allah; they are constantly moving in the inner garden of the pure heart.

'Those who restrain their anger and pardon men': this does not mean that they do not experience anger: anger is a creational attribute, and in itself is not a harmful quality. The Qur'an does say, however, that those who guard themselves – the devout ones – do not misplace their anger, but rather hold on to it and allow it to manifest itself in a positive way and in the way of Allah. Those who do not restrain their anger simply react in a quick-tempered manner and dissipate their energy in an emotional way.

The root of the word 'pardon' (*'afw*, عفو) literally means 'to obliterate what has happened, erase the trace of an action, forget or cover it'. In the context of the Qur'an, it means those who lean towards others with compassion. We must have compassion for a person who makes mistakes. 'And Allah loves those who do good.' We must incline towards other people kindly, for that is the way of excellent action (*iḥsān*, إحسان). Amongst Muslims there are always those who cannot deal with controversy and confrontation. Allah commands us to have mercy upon the weak and meek, as we shall see in the next verse.

The truly pious person spends money on others 'in ease as well as in adversity', sometimes anonymously and at other times publicly. 'Those who spend their wealth by night and day, secretly and openly, shall have their reward from their Lord, and they shall have no fear, neither shall they grieve' (2: 274). A devout person is generous in all situations. To develop generosity is to break the lower, human tendency of greed and fear of lack of provision. It is incumbent upon us to sever ourselves from all that we depend upon.

These are ways towards the station of excellence (*maqām al-iḥsān*, مقام الإحسان), acting from the knowledge that although we do not see it, Allah is behind everything. He sees us, for He is the All-Seeing. These are the ways towards spontaneous and constant awareness and remembrance (*dhikr*, ذكر).

وَالَّذِينَ إِذَا فَعَلُوا فَاحِشَةً أَوْ ظَلَمُوٓا أَنْفُسَهُمْ ذَكَرُوا
اللَّهَ فَاسْتَغْفَرُوا لِذُنُوبِهِمْ وَمَنْ يَغْفِرُ الذُّنُوبَ إِلَّا
اللَّهُ وَلَمْ يُصِرُّوا عَلَىٰ مَا فَعَلُوا وَهُمْ يَعْلَمُونَ

135 **And those who when they do something wrong or do an injustice to themselves remember Allah, ask forgiveness for their faults – who forgives faults except Allah – and do not knowingly persist in what they have done.**

The ultimate wrongdoing (*fāḥish'ah*, فَاحِشَة) is disbelief (*kufr*, كُفر) in Allah and unity (*tawḥīd*, تَوحيد). One who commits an indecency against himself, but then remembers Allah and returns to the path of Allah seeking forgiveness, will receive His forgiveness. Allah can forgive our mistakes, because this life is the training-ground for the next life, and now is the time allotted for learning from our errors.

'And who do not knowingly persist in what they have done': forgiveness occurs when we recognize our error and desist from repeating our mistakes. If we consciously repeat our mistakes, we can neither be protected nor forgiven. The believer does not commit the same error twice, for once he becomes aware of its origin, he avoids the trap and moves on, enriched.

أُولَٰئِكَ جَزَاؤُهُم مَّغْفِرَةٌ مِّن رَّبِّهِمْ وَجَنَّاتٌ تَجْرِي
مِن تَحْتِهَا الْأَنْهَارُ خَالِدِينَ فِيهَا ۚ وَنِعْمَ أَجْرُ الْعَامِلِينَ

136 Their reward is forgiveness from their Lord and gardens beneath which rivers flow, abiding in them forever. What an excellent reward for those who labour!

For those who avoid what has caused them affliction is the reward of forgiveness and the Garden of ease and harmony, fed by unseen rivers. The reward is wholesomeness, contentment, remembrance and awareness. If a person of faith knows what he is doing and why he is doing it, he cannot fail to be balanced and poised with a high expectation of Allah's mercy.

قَدْ خَلَتْ مِن قَبْلِكُمْ سُنَنٌ فَسِيرُوا فِي
الْأَرْضِ فَانظُرُوا كَيْفَ كَانَ عَاقِبَةُ الْمُكَذِّبِينَ

137 Indeed, there have been examples before you, so travel in the earth and see what was the end of those who rejected.

The way of Allah does not change. Examples of man's arrogance, which leads to the rejection of what is true, have surfaced in every time and place. The people who came before had their paths to follow, and the path of Islam is to follow the Prophet and refrain from disagreement, which only results in loss and dispersion, preventing mankind from building a community in which real knowledge and enlightenment can take root. The Qur'an tells us to travel in the land and see how many cultures better than ours have been destroyed, to explore for the sake of knowledge. Peoples and nations of the past deviated from the laws of Allah and were therefore destroyed. The fact that the Muslims were with the Prophet at Uḥud did not prevent their defeat, for they failed to obey him.

هَٰذَا بَيَانٌ لِّلنَّاسِ وَهُدًى وَمَوْعِظَةٌ لِّلْمُتَّقِينَ

138 This is a clear statement to mankind, a guidance and an admonition to those who would guard cautiously.

The Qur'an is Allah's final revealed message to humankind, and is a clear proof containing guidance and exhortation for those who have perception. 'O Prophet! Surely We have sent you as a witness, as a bearer of good news, as a warner, as one inviting to Allah by His permission, and as a shining light' (33: 44-46).

Each one of us witnesses. All of mankind shares one common

experience, one process. At first we witness our own troubles, afflictions and desires. The years which we experience are similar in meaning to those years experienced by the Muslims of Mecca and Medina. We experience doubt and certainty as they did, and we too receive the good news about the source of existence which permeates all-existential experience. With this good news, however, comes the news concerning limitations. The boundaries are made clear and caution is the byword. The worst thing that can happen to a person is that he begins to see the truth and thinks that he can sneak around it. This is a very dangerous condition. 'What! Do they then feel secure from Allah's plans? But none feels secure from Allah's plans except the people who perish' (7: 99).

Man must be wary, for Allah will lead him to the edge whether he is strong enough or not, in order to create strength in him. He must not think that he is safe because he has attained some knowledge and power. The more knowledge one has, the greater the extent of the failure. The mistake of a man with intellect and wisdom is a big one for he can lead an entire community astray, whereas one who is alone leads only himself astray. The more influence a person exercises, the more evident the mistakes will be.

'An admonition to those who guard cautiously': we are urged by a warning to look in the direction of the light-giving star (*sirāj munīr*, سِرَاج مُنِير), to be guided by that light, and not to wander off into the darkness. That is, we must not do anything unless the reasons for the action are clear. What is done in darkness and confusion will surely fail to be of value. Others simply close their eyes and plunge on. We are given the freedom to drown in our ignorance or rise by the guiding light. Once we realize our essential reality we must not waste a moment.

'Surely Hell lies in wait' (78: 21). The inner state of fire and agitation is continuously on the look-out for those who are astray. A person whose focus is not upon Allah is in darkness and without direction. We come into Hell's sight when we do not use our

confined or restricted, when he begins to possess the accoutrements of this world. When the believers were gathered around the Prophet, free from worldly attachments, they were far better off than after attaining success in this world.

وَمَا مُحَمَّدٌ إِلَّا رَسُولٌ قَدْ خَلَتْ مِن قَبْلِهِ الرُّسُلُ
أَفَإِن مَّاتَ أَوْ قُتِلَ انقَلَبْتُمْ عَلَىٰ أَعْقَابِكُمْ
وَمَن يَنقَلِبْ عَلَىٰ عَقِبَيْهِ فَلَن يَضُرَّ اللَّهَ شَيْئًا
وَسَيَجْزِي اللَّهُ الشَّاكِرِينَ

144 **And Muhammad is only a messenger. Messengers have passed away before him. If he then dies or is killed, will you turn back upon your heels? And whoever turns back upon his heels will by no means do harm to Allah. And Allah will reward the grateful.**

All the messengers have been tested and afflicted by Allah's creation, and all have been obedient to them. This verse tells us not to attribute to the Prophet more than Allah has attributed to him. He is like all the others who were carriers of a message.

'If then he dies or is killed, will you turn back upon your heels?' One must be aware of the words and the order in which they occur, because the Qur'an is very precise. The believers are asked if they will retreat upon the Prophet's death, foreshadowing what was truly to befall Islam after the death of the Prophet.

When the Battle of Uḥud ended, only 'Alī and one other Companion remained with the Prophet. According to the traditions, about twelve people defended the Prophet, but the rest of them were killed. The majority of these twelve were from Medina, having joined the Prophet after the migration. They had been with him only a short time. This illustrates the fact that there was no necessary merit in the number of years a companion was with the Prophet. The Prophet himself remarked that some people who had never seen him were closer to his heart than some of the Companions around him. To follow the Prophet brings knowledge and a sense of unity, so no doubt those who were with him longer benefited more. However the vast majority of Arabs who embraced Islam during the last few years of the Prophet's life in Medina were simply fellow travellers.

'And whoever turns back upon his heels will by no means do harm to Allah.' The laws of Allah will prevail. The message of divine unity and its application will inevitably come to people; this is an inescapable truth. Only the person who recognizes and submits to the truth does himself justice.

وَمَا كَانَ لِنَفْسٍ أَنْ تَمُوتَ إِلَّا بِإِذْنِ اللَّهِ كِتَابًا
مُؤَجَّلًا وَمَنْ يُرِدْ ثَوَابَ الدُّنْيَا نُؤْتِهِ مِنْهَا وَمَنْ يُرِدْ ثَوَابَ
الْآخِرَةِ نُؤْتِهِ مِنْهَا وَسَنَجْزِي الشَّاكِرِينَ

145 No soul dies except with Allah's permission; everyone's term is fixed. Whoever desires and strives for the reward of this world, We shall give it to him; while whoever desires and strives for the reward of the Hereafter, We shall give it to him. We will reward the grateful.

The term of man's life in this world is fixed. Bound within the realm of time, it is our destiny to die without knowing beforehand when the moment of death or its attendant conditions will come. The knowledge of these lies with Allah alone,Who is beyond measurable time. This verse encourages people always to strive spiritually, since they do not know when the moment of death and inaction will come. The only option we have is to seek for knowledge of unity, accepting and submitting to our destiny, for the final outcome of our lives is in Allah's hands.

'And whoever wants and strives for ... We shall give it to him.' The person who wants this world, as well as the person who truly desires spiritual knowledge, will eventually get what they desire. Existence has its rules, and by following them meticulously one will gain the object of one's desires. These rules apply in all instances of the desire to attain, whether these desires are worthy or mundane.

'And We will reward the grateful' is a phrase that is repeated often in the Qur'an. True reward comes to those who are in a state of gratefulness (*shukr*, شُكر), for this state begets the optimum degree of efficiency. This verse and the one that precedes it complement and reinforce each other. Those who are in this state of gratefulness will obtain a double reward: being able to recognize things as they are, to see the perfection of creational laws; and obtaining what they had set out to obtain. They will be successful in every way, in their knowledge and also in meeting with their own destiny, which they experience as being in harmony with the decree of Allah.

وَكَأَيِّن مِّن نَّبِيٍّ قَاتَلَ مَعَهُ رِبِّيُّونَ كَثِيرٌ فَمَا
وَهَنُوا لِمَا أَصَابَهُمْ فِي سَبِيلِ اللَّهِ وَمَا ضَعُفُوا
وَمَا اسْتَكَانُوا وَاللَّهُ يُحِبُّ الصَّابِرِينَ

146 How many a prophet has fought, and many worshippers of the Lord were with him. They did not become weak-hearted on account of what befell them in Allah's way, nor did they submit or surrender. Allah loves the patient.

It has always been the case that those who are close to the original transmitters of knowledge (who are the prophets of Allah) are amongst those who believe most firmly in their Lord. They believe in being raised by divine guidance to fulfil their potential. They trust wholeheartedly that everything which comes to them is from Reality, thus they interact with every event in an appropriate way. They are loyal to their belief in His lordship, and are thus loyal to those whom they befriend and support. They are steadfast and courageous. A way of knowing who one's true friends are is to observe how people around one act when one is in difficulty. The moment the Muslims abandoned the field of battle for the lure of booty, Khalid ibn al-Walid and the enemy came down upon them. The majority of the Muslims ran for cover, and most of those who stood their ground were killed. 'And Allah loves the patient.' The verbal root of 'the patient' also means 'to bind, tie, shackle'. Those who are patient are bound inextricably to the truth.

وَمَا كَانَ قَوْلَهُمْ إِلَّا أَن قَالُوا رَبَّنَا اغْفِرْ لَنَا ذُنُوبَنَا
وَإِسْرَافَنَا فِي أَمْرِنَا وَثَبِّتْ أَقْدَامَنَا وَانصُرْنَا عَلَى الْقَوْمِ الْكَافِرِينَ

147 And they said: Our Lord, forgive our faults and our extravagance in our affair; make our feet firm, and help us against the unbelieving people.

Those who are in true abandonment and in the way of Allah are steadfast; they are the elect of the elite. They are the peopleof true spirituality. Their supplication is for forgiveness (*ghufrān*, غُفْرَان). They have realized that even one moment spent in anything other than a state of unity is 'extravagance' (*israf*, إِسْرَاف). They ask to be made firm in faith, that their faith might gain dominance over denial.

فَآتَاهُمُ اللَّهُ ثَوَابَ الدُّنْيَا وَحُسْنَ ثَوَابِ الْآخِرَةِ
وَاللَّهُ يُحِبُّ الْمُحْسِنِينَ

148 So Allah gave them the reward of this world, and better, the reward of the Hereafter. Allah loves those who do good.

Those who are in a true state of faith, and who translate that faith first into the purification of intention and then into appropriate action, will surely meet with success here and now. Their actions also predetermine their success in the next life where there is no longer an opportunity for action nor is there any apparent freedom. The freedom to act, which we apparently have in this world, is a kind of licence enabling us to recognize that, in truth, when we act in the most efficient and harmonious way we have no choice but to act in a certain prescribed way. The word freedom implies multiple choices, and therefore possible confusion and failure. He who knows what needs to be done in order to succeed has no choice or freedom but to act in a specific way. Men of knowledge have always known that the more knowledge one has, the less freedom one has.

The more one knows about the self, the more one understands the danger of denial and hypocrisy, the less choice one has. Freedom in having less choice actually means freedom from ignorance, which implies that one is tethered and restricted by knowledge. In our time, however, to be free means to live with one's ignorance; we see the outcome of this kind of freedom in the severe ills of modern society.

يَا أَيُّهَا الَّذِينَ آمَنُوا إِن تُطِيعُوا الَّذِينَ كَفَرُوا
يَرُدُّوكُمْ عَلَىٰ أَعْقَابِكُمْ
فَتَنقَلِبُوا خَاسِرِينَ

149 O you who believe, if you obey those who disbelieve, they will turn you back upon your heels, and you will be losers.

Several commentators mention that this verse is a reference to Abū Sufyān, the leader of the Quraysh at the Battle of Uḥud, and to his chief lieutenant, Khālid ibn al-Walīd.

Among the believers, different degrees of faith and different capabilities for translating that faith into intention and action are to be found. The strength of faith in a person generally fluctuates until it becomes firmly established, then it becomes rooted and certain. All believers may be affected by doubt and weakness until their hearts are strengthened with faith and knowledge of Allah. This process was proven by the events at Uḥud.

بَلِ اللَّهُ مَوْلَاكُمْ ۖ وَهُوَ خَيْرُ النَّاصِرِينَ

150 But Allah is your protector and He is the best of helpers.

The one who witnesses, experiences and befriends Reality will want neither for another friend nor another power. One whose faith is deep, and whose knowledge has increased with time and events, has taken Allah as his Protector and Master (*Mawlā*, مَوْلَى). This person is in truth always victorious, even though appearances may suggest his defeat. Even though it appeared that the Prophet had lost at Uḥud, his apparent loss was in reality a victory, for those around him gained knowledge of the degree of their weakness, and future generations gained the example of Uḥud which enabled them to perceive the weaknesses of their own hearts. One cannot but feel joy at seeing Allah's laws at work, or at feeling the compassion Allah has placed in us for those who are weak in faith.

For the true believer, the realization that the laws of Allah are always operative is like being safely anchored in a stormy sea. It is the duty of man to act for his own benefit with responsibility and understanding. 'This is because Allah has never changed a favour which He has conferred upon a people until they change their own condition' (8: 53). We must be given a length of rope with which to manoeuvre and test ourselves, so that we may finally discover that, in fact, this very rope is the way to freedom, the freedom of abandonment and acceptance of Allah's laws.

سَنُلْقِي فِي قُلُوبِ الَّذِينَ كَفَرُوا الرُّعْبَ بِمَا
أَشْرَكُوا بِاللَّهِ مَا لَمْ يُنَزِّلْ بِهِ سُلْطَانًا ۖ
وَمَأْوَاهُمُ النَّارُ ۚ وَبِئْسَ مَثْوَى الظَّالِمِينَ

151 We will cast terror into the hearts of those who disbelieve, because they associated with Allah that for which He has revealed no authority; and their abode is the Fire. Evil is the dwelling place of the unjust.

Fear comes to the heart according to the degree of doubt and disbelief. If a man really denies the truth of Reality and believes neither in unity (*tawḥīd*, تَوْحِيد) nor in the Hereafter, he will flee from confrontation with the truth because of fear of death. The heart of a believer (*mu'min*, مُؤْمِن) not yet firmly anchored will also experience fear. In this case, however, it is an opportunity to move towards deeper faith. The believer's fear challenges him to rise up, whereas the non-believer's fear only imprisons him further.

The outer implication of this verse is directed towards the people of Uḥud. It tells them not to worry about their loss. It explains that fear will always come to the heart of those who are not confirmed in faith, because they believe neither in Allah nor in the next life. Even though the man of disbelief may seem fearless, he is undeniably afraid of death.

وَلَقَدْ صَدَقَكُمُ اللَّهُ وَعْدَهُ إِذْ تَحُسُّونَهُمْ
بِإِذْنِهِ ۖ حَتَّىٰ إِذَا فَشِلْتُمْ وَتَنَازَعْتُمْ فِي الْأَمْرِ وَعَصَيْتُمْ
مِنْ بَعْدِ مَا أَرَاكُمْ مَا تُحِبُّونَ ۚ مِنْكُمْ مَنْ يُرِيدُ الدُّنْيَا
وَمِنْكُمْ مَنْ يُرِيدُ الْآخِرَةَ ۚ ثُمَّ صَرَفَكُمْ عَنْهُمْ لِيَبْتَلِيَكُمْ ۖ
وَلَقَدْ عَفَا عَنْكُمْ ۗ وَاللَّهُ ذُو فَضْلٍ عَلَى الْمُؤْمِنِينَ

152 **And certainly Allah fulfilled His promise to you when you routed them by His permission, until you became weak-hearted, disputed about the affair, and disobeyed after He had shown you that which you love. Among you were some who desired this world, and among you were some who desired the Hereafter. Then He turned you away from them that He might try you, and He has certainly pardoned you. Allah is gracious to the believers.**

The Battle of Uḥud is a battle which never ends; we participate in it every moment of our lives. At the very beginning of the battle the Muslims were united, obedient to their leader, and without fear. Doubt, dispute and greed dissolved their unity and strength. The fifty men whom the Prophet had strategically placed began to listen to the voice of the lower self and to agitation. Shayṭān operates within the heart of man; in the Qur'an many references equate *Shayṭān* with man when the lower tendency takes over human action.

During times of difficulty and hardship one discovers deeper elements within oneself, as well as what one's priorities are. Usually a man who has no material possessions can, with little effort, abstain from worldly desires and wealth. This same person, however, when taken to the market and given a blank cheque to spend will soon discover his greed and covetousness. Here Allah is saying to the believers that among the few hundred people who accompanied the Prophet, and who were the best among those called 'the Companions', were many who loved material possessions and booty more than self-sacrifice in the way of Allah.

Some of the great commentators defined 'the Companions' as those who had seen the Prophet. The verbal root of 'companions' (*ṣaḥābah*, صَحَابة) also means 'to accompany'. Historically, the word refers to those who were physically with the Prophet, but it also implies they were with him inwardly as well as outwardly. We are informed that at Uḥud only two men remained with the Prophet at the end of the battle. We must reflect upon this event and its implications and not assume that all 'Companions' were real and close to the prophetic path.

This verse, along with the following few, are a detailed description of the Battle of Uḥud, a battle that lives on as an existential reality at all times. We could easily become cowards and lose our ground because of disputes and doubts which result in confusion, eventually leading us to destruction. In our lives, the battle may be played out in ways which seem insignificant until we realize the dimensions of their consequences. We may lose the battle when, for instance, rather than helping a person in need, we speak disparagingly about him and cast doubts into the hearts of others about him. Allah has said,

'Among you were some who desired this world (*dunyā*, دُنْيَا) and among you were some who desired the Hereafter (*Ākhirah*, آخِرَة).' When our love of the world wins out over our love for the unseen world of the Hereafter, then we have lost.

Somehow the people of Uḥud were saved from being completely annihilated: under the circumstances, the Muslims suffered few losses, many succeeding in escaping with their lives. Since the enemy numbered 3,000, it was, in a way, a great success that only about seventy Muslim men were killed.

'Then He turned you away from them that He might try you.' A test is truly a blessing which causes us to reflect upon the meaning of our experiences and the extent of our weaknesses and strengths. It is the love of Allah for the believer which allows him to witness himself. If he did not bear witness upon himself in this world, he would be faced with his inner veils, self-deception and hypocrisy.

'And He has certainly pardoned you.' Those who are sincere in their quest for truth will be given another chance to travel upward on the path of spiritual growth. This verse is directed at believers, who will understand the degree to which they have allowed their lower tendencies to rule over them.

إِذْ تُصْعِدُونَ وَلَا تَلْوُۥنَ عَلَىٰٓ أَحَدٍ وَٱلرَّسُولُ
يَدْعُوكُمْ فِىٓ أُخْرَىٰكُمْ فَأَثَٰبَكُمْ غَمًّۢا
بِغَمٍّ لِّكَيْلَا تَحْزَنُوا۟ عَلَىٰ مَا فَاتَكُمْ
وَلَا مَآ أَصَٰبَكُمْ ۗ وَٱللَّهُ خَبِيرٌۢ بِمَا تَعْمَلُونَ

153 When you ran off and paid no heed, and the Messenger was calling you from behind. He gave you distress upon distress, that you might not grieve at what had escaped you, and nor at what befell you. Allah is aware of what you do.

The Qur'an continues with more detailed description of the events at Uḥud. We know that among the followers of the Prophet, or any community led by men of knowledge, when seemingly insurmountable difficulties arise, the weak are overwhelmed and flee. This desire to escape results from a lack of knowledge, wisdom and inner steadfastness.

We are all afraid to look inside ourselves, in case we hear the voice of prophetic truth which will embarrass us. We do not wish to hear anything that will deter us in our efforts to escape from apparent outer difficulty. 'And the Messenger was calling you from behind. He gave you distress upon distress.' Here Allah says that as a result of not listening, of running away and attempting to avoid the problem – actions which show a lack of both certitude and faith – the reward is 'distress upon distress'. We have all had occasions when we wished to sever our ties with a man to whom we had pledged our support, or when we wished to renounce the truth we had vowed to uphold.

One distress (*ghamm*, غمّ) is the grief they felt because of their perceived weakness and loss. The second distress was because they had wronged others. The Muslims at Uḥud grieved over what they had done to their Prophet, for they returned to find him wounded, with 'Alī, also wounded, beside him. The reward of weak faith and no discipline is double grief. This event was given to them not as a punishment, but to show them the laws of action and reaction at work. Each person must learn to observe Allah's natural decree at work in his own life by observing his own sorrow and distress.

'That you might not grieve at what had escaped you nor be anxious at what befell you': this is the heart of the matter: the Muslims are told not to experience emotional grief over their physical losses. The believer is in no distress over what has passed. He derives only benefit from events around him, because he reflects upon them and thereby derives knowledge. 'There is no stopping-place for the people of Medina', as the tradition tells us. They move on. This is the way (*Sunnah*, سُنَّة) of the Prophet Muhammad.

We often speak about the way of the Prophet, about the message and the messenger, but do we really fully understand what these descriptions mean, and do we know how to benefit from them? The verse says, 'That you might not grieve'. Sorrow comes essentially from a situation which is out of balance or harmony. Clarity can only come about when the why and how of a thing are known precisely. Grief, therefore, implies ignorance. Allah wants the believers to recognize the benefit to be derived from what has happened to them, so that they will not grieve superficially over the loss of some material object. He also wants them to understand that what has occurred to them is in fact a manifestation of Allah's decree, mercy and justice.

The Companions were clearly successful in this world and the next when they obeyed the Prophet at Badr. At Uḥud, however, they transgressed, and the result was temporary loss and regret. The Qur'an counsels them not to grieve but to see instead the meaning and benefit, so that the same mistake is not repeated. One never repeats a mistake if one has truly recognized its cause, and has resolved to be on guard against repeating the error. For example, if a child receives only a slight electric shock from touching an exposed wire, he may not become sufficiently aware of the danger of his action. If he receives a violent shock, however, he will remember never to touch the wire again, because he will have fully understood the meaning of his action.

'And Allah is aware of what you do.' Allah knows all of our actions and He also knows of our need to have access to knowledge. Indeed Allah is the source of all creation. Access to real knowledge is obtained through access to one's inner being. We must not only grieve over wrong acts in themselves, rather, we must take personal responsibility and grieve over our continuous heedlessness. If our grief is real, we will not forget Allah, because real grief brings about remembrance and the desire to be fully awakened. This is the lesson of Uḥud. Every moment and every situation is Uḥud or Karbala (the desert where Imam Husayn was martyred). These are not past events simply to be commemorated ceremoniously. Remembrance has no value if the lessons are not applied to our own lives.

ثُمَّ أَنزَلَ عَلَيْكُم مِّن بَعْدِ الْغَمِّ أَمَنَةً نُّعَاسًا يَغْشَىٰ طَائِفَةً مِّنكُمْ
وَطَائِفَةٌ قَدْ أَهَمَّتْهُمْ أَنفُسُهُمْ يَظُنُّونَ بِاللَّهِ غَيْرَ الْحَقِّ ظَنَّ
الْجَاهِلِيَّةِ يَقُولُونَ هَل لَّنَا مِنَ الْأَمْرِ مِن شَيْءٍ قُلْ إِنَّ الْأَمْرَ كُلَّهُ
لِلَّهِ يُخْفُونَ فِي أَنفُسِهِم مَّا لَا يُبْدُونَ لَكَ يَقُولُونَ لَوْ كَانَ
لَنَا مِنَ الْأَمْرِ شَيْءٌ مَّا قُتِلْنَا هَاهُنَا قُل لَّوْ كُنتُمْ فِي بُيُوتِكُمْ
لَبَرَزَ الَّذِينَ كُتِبَ عَلَيْهِمُ الْقَتْلُ إِلَىٰ مَضَاجِعِهِمْ وَلِيَبْتَلِيَ
اللَّهُ مَا فِي صُدُورِكُمْ وَلِيُمَحِّصَ مَا فِي قُلُوبِكُمْ
وَاللَّهُ عَلِيمٌ بِذَاتِ الصُّدُورِ

154 After distress He made you secure, and a drowsiness enveloped some of you. Others were filled with anxiety, for they entertained ignorant thoughts about Allah. They were saying: We have no hand in the affair. Say: Surely the affair is completely Allah's. They conceal within themselves what they would not reveal to you. They say: Had we any hand in the affair, we would not have been slain here. Say: Had you remained in your houses, those for whom death was ordained would certainly have gone forth to the place where they would be slain. Allah tests what is in your hearts that He might purge what is therein. Allah is the knower of what the hearts contain.

During the Battle of Uḥud, seeds of doubt were sown in the hearts of the weak believers by the voice of the *Shayṭān* calling them to loot, and later spreading the rumour that the Prophet had been killed. The Muslims did not want to hear the higher voice of self-sacrifice because it challenged them too greatly, so instead, they listened to the lower whispers. Many of the Muslims thought that during the Battle of Uḥud the Prophet had died and the battle was over, and that therefore there was no longer any reason to stand and fight. Then they sought to appease the enemy.

'After distress He sent down security upon you, a drowsiness enveloping a party of you.' The party referred to here could have been the group of Companions who had fought with all their strength. These believers, who were totally committed, were in the middle of the battle when suddenly events began to turn; during the lull they were overcome by drowsiness. It is said that their heads fell upon their chests as though slumber had overtaken them (i.e. to allow them to recover). Another party 'who were filled with anxiety' were worrying about themselves: they were the Muslims who possessed a low degree of faith.

'They entertained ignorant thoughts about Allah.' That is, they did not truly understand the way of Allah. The Prophet said, 'Reflect upon the creation of Allah and do not reflect upon Allah.' How is it possible to think of Allah? The moment we think about Allah we fall into illusion. Rather, we should think of Allah's creation and the intricate, balanced, and perfect laws that govern the creation. We should reflect upon the equal and opposite character of action and reaction, and of the relation of cause and effect. We should think of the beauty, balance and magnificence of the creation. It is no use speculating about Allah, for it is existence and creation that point to Allah, the Creator.

They entertained thoughts about Allah that were not true, because they did not know the laws of Allah. They thought that because they were with the Prophet, a magical change in their condition would take place. They did not realize that they would have to make an effort in order to achieve success. Allah's creation exists to show us the meaning of oneness and the intricate interplay of its many facets. Allah seems to be saying that we cannot rely simply on wishful thinking and superstition. We need to learn how to strive for ourselves, and interact with the world for desirable results. In the Battle of Uḥud the Prophet did not lose his life and, through his faith and patience, was able to reverse the course of events. 'Alī the Prophet's Companion, defended him by fighting off twenty men, thus saving the Prophet's life. The meaning of Reality is demonstrated to us in manifestation as a field in which we can act. By the use of our intellect we can come to understand that the man who is not afraid of death is equal to many other men in battle who are scared. Doubt will sabotage the weak, and the strong of heart will always win.

By his very nature man wants success; therefore, failure implies ignorance in the form of wrong application, wrong timing, cowardice, greed or any other of ignorance's myriad forms. We must not disavow our responsibility, saying that we did not know how to act. On the contrary, the whole affair is our responsibility, and the fault is entirely ours. Trouble comes from us and mercy comes from Allah. Mercy issues from laws that are immutable. We must recognize these laws in order to apply them, and to live dynamically within their protection. In this way we will come to know the meaning of true abandonment and the realm beyond time and space.

'They say: Had we any hand in the affair, we would not have been slain here.' This is the voice exclaiming fear of death. Before the battle the hypocrites (*munāfiqūn*, مُنَافِقُون) could be heard discouraging the Muslims. Today many Muslims say that fighting in the way of Allah is a thing of the past and is not appropriate to this time. A person may easily justify his failure to pursue a vigorous path of struggle against his ego-self. If his faith is weak, he will hear voices that weaken him further still.

The hypocrites disclaimed their responsibility for desertion by claiming that they saw others wounded and running and thus had to flee. They claimed additionally to have no responsibility for the loss incurred, stating that all events come from Allah and He did not want them to win. Yet Allah says in the Qur'an that He does not change the condition of a people unless they change themselves. Man ignorantly blames Allah for what has befallen him, because he does not know the nature of Reality.

Uḥud presented an opportunity for the Muslims to reflect upon their intentions and actions. The one whose intentions are exposed is fortunate, because he can see the hidden machinations of his ego-self and is thereby given the opportunity to change and progress. For example, if we recognize that betrayal is a predominant element in our nature, we experience greater awareness of that tendency and can more easily overcome it. The same is true on a physical level: if we recognize that our actions are erratic due to a physical imbalance, we are able to make an allowance. Recognizing our times of weakness neutralizes the extent of their affliction.

'Say: Had you remained in your houses' is a reply to the Jews and others in Medina who told the believers that had they stayed in their homes, the Muslims would not have been killed. The battle of life is upon us 'that Allah might test what was in your hearts'. The word for a test or trial (*balā'*, بَلاء) also means 'to wear down'. The nature of Allah's love is to reveal what is in our hearts in order to wear out or relieve the sickness therein. In this way, the veils that prevent us from experiencing unity within ourselves are stripped away, and we are able to act in harmony with what is innermost in our hearts. Allah 'wears out' what is in the breast so the heart is rendered pure and free. Thus, we are permitted to return to the Source within us.

'And Allah knows what is in the hearts.' Self-knowledge comes from Allah; it is an intimate, special relationship. Incumbent upon each of us is to take part in the Battle of Uḥud, to lose and yet win, as the Muslims did there. At that time, it became clear who were the true believers and who were hypocrites.

إِنَّ الَّذِينَ تَوَلَّوْا مِنكُمْ يَوْمَ الْتَقَى الْجَمْعَانِ إِنَّمَا
اسْتَزَلَّهُمُ الشَّيْطَانُ بِبَعْضِ مَا كَسَبُوا وَلَقَدْ عَفَا
اللَّهُ عَنْهُمْ إِنَّ اللَّهَ غَفُورٌ حَلِيمٌ

155 Surely, those of you who turned back on the day when the two hosts met, were caused to slip by Shayṭān because of what they had done, but Allah has pardoned them. Surely, Allah is Forgiving, Forbearing.

Those of weak faith (*īmān*, إيمان), that is, the majority of the Muslims, ran when 'the two armies met'. The little they had earned materially and spiritually was not enough. A little knowledge is dangerous, because it can easily slip from one's grasp. An analogy of the process of awakening to knowledge is the child's ability to reason: the child does not immediately understand a whole situation. Similarly, most Muslims take only a small part of the life-transaction (*dīn*, دين) that is Islam, the part which is most convenient for them to use. Since we love the world, we support our materialistic tendencies by quoting traditions that describe how Allah prefers a stronger, wealthier Muslim to a poorer one. We fail to remember, however, that throughout the entire Qur'an, giving and spending are always emphasized, and greed and accumulated wealth are discouraged. The Qur'an says that Allah will give us our provision (*rizq*, رزق) from whence we know not.

'Surely, Allah is Forgiving, Forbearing.' The dominating message of this verse is that Allah will forgive those who are sincere in their quest, and He will rejuvenate them to act once again with greater knowledge.

يَا أَيُّهَا الَّذِينَ آمَنُوا لَا تَكُونُوا كَالَّذِينَ كَفَرُوا وَقَالُوا
لِإِخْوَانِهِمْ إِذَا ضَرَبُوا فِي الْأَرْضِ أَوْ كَانُوا غُزًّى لَوْ كَانُوا عِنْدَنَا
مَا مَاتُوا وَمَا قُتِلُوا لِيَجْعَلَ اللَّهُ ذَٰلِكَ حَسْرَةً فِي
قُلُوبِهِمْ ۗ وَاللَّهُ يُحْيِي وَيُمِيتُ ۗ وَاللَّهُ بِمَا تَعْمَلُونَ بَصِيرٌ

156 O you who believe, do not be like those who disbelieve and say of their brethren when they travel in the earth or engage in fighting: Had they remained with us, they would not have died nor would they have been slain; for Allah will cause you to regret such an attitude. Allah grants life and causes death, and Allah sees what you do.

Those who believe are not like those who disbelieve. This verse tells those who believe not to follow the non-believers in their uncertainty, doubts and confusion. Those who want to be stronger in their belief must not fall into this trap. The believers must not look back in regret.

The words 'they would not have died nor would they have been slain' clearly indicate their defiance. How can anyone say that if others had not gone into battle they would have remained alive? Circumstances can change at any moment. In this sense, man can never fully predict matters in an empirical way.

وَلَئِنْ قُتِلْتُمْ فِي سَبِيلِ اللَّهِ أَوْ مُتُّمْ لَمَغْفِرَةٌ
مِنَ اللَّهِ وَرَحْمَةٌ خَيْرٌ مِمَّا يَجْمَعُونَ

157 If you are slain in the way of Allah or you die, certainly forgiveness from Allah and mercy are better than what they collect.

وَلَئِن مُّتُّمْ أَوْ قُتِلْتُمْ لَإِلَى اللَّهِ تُحْشَرُونَ

158 **And if you die or you are slain, certainly to Allah you shall be gathered.**

In verse 157, being slain (*qutila*, قُتِلَ) is mentioned before dying. This indicates that willingness to die in martyrdom is better than passively accepting death. If a person is killed in the way of Allah, having abandoned himself to Him is better than all that he has attained on earth. It is better for him than the wealth of a kingdom, because having died for Allah is the key to eternal freedom; he is honoured as the guest of the King of kings in a state of boundlessness. The people who chase after possessions merely collect a few trinkets.

By mentioning being killed before natural death, Allah is making a statement regarding the sacrifice of man for the sake of truth. He is saying that the one who is willing to abandon his most valuable possession, that is, his life, is indeed with Allah.

فَبِمَا رَحْمَةٍ مِّنَ اللَّهِ لِنتَ لَهُمْ وَلَوْ كُنتَ فَظًّا غَلِيظَ الْقَلْبِ
لَانفَضُّوا مِنْ حَوْلِكَ فَاعْفُ عَنْهُمْ وَاسْتَغْفِرْ لَهُمْ
وَشَاوِرْهُمْ فِي الْأَمْرِ فَإِذَا عَزَمْتَ فَتَوَكَّلْ عَلَى
اللَّهِ إِنَّ اللَّهَ يُحِبُّ الْمُتَوَكِّلِينَ

159 **So it is by mercy from Allah that you deal with them gently. Had you been rough and hard-hearted, they would certainly have dispersed from around you. So pardon them, ask forgiveness for them, and take counsel with them in the affair. And when you have decided, then place your trust in Allah. Surely, Allah loves those who trust.**

Gentleness is an Attribute of Allah that we wish to cultivate. It was an attribute of the perfect leader whom we wish to follow through the portals of the Garden. If the Prophet had not been of such high character, had his heart not been so compassionate, people would not have flocked to Islam. The Qur'an implies that ingrained in every heart is the desire to strive after the highest of values. Once the believer sees these values clearly manifested, he will, according to his strength or weakness, seek them.

Then Allah addresses the Prophet saying, 'Pardon them.' We can forgive someone for ourselves, but we cannot extend forgiveness on behalf of others, and we cannot compensate for someone's wrong actions against Allah. We may forgive someone for having damaged our crop, but we cannot forgive him on behalf of nature for having damaged its environment. A person's actions must cause natural reactions. Because of the loftiness of our nature, we may forgive others in the same way as the prophets did. 'And ask forgiveness for them': the Prophet is asked to pray for an end to their weakness, so that they may be forgiven.

'And take counsel with them.' This is the foundational element of a community: the sharing of reasoning and sound thought with one another. The leader should consult the people before he acts, although he may sometimes find them weak and unable to follow through. To consult with someone does not necessarily imply following their recommendations, it simply implies interaction, inquiry and the choice of the best course. Prophetic leadership is not democratic in the narrow, secular sense.

The Qur'an continues, 'When you have decided', that is, when one has collected all the information by consulting and listening, then one makes a clear decision. Allah loves those who are decisive. He loves those who use their intellect, who expect the best and act accordingly without wavering. 'Allah loves those who trust.' Once a decision has been made, action is to be taken.

'Do men think that they will be left alone on saying, 'We

believe, and will not be tried?' (29: 2) We will be afflicted with weakness and with doubts. The steadfast and patient man will stand like a beacon upon the shore; nothing moves him. Though the waves crash against him, he stands his ground. He is decisive and certain because he knows that ultimately victory comes from Allah, and that what he represents will prevail although this may not be instantly apparent. The killing of a prophet does not stop the message. We cannot win by merely disposing of someone who opposes us, particularly if that person represents the truth, for it remains ready to reappear, perhaps in the next generation. The truth is that man will not rest until he knows the purpose of his creation, and he will not know until he is certain and secure in his faith and submission. Man will never be satisfied with any amount of material wealth until he is certain in his heart about Allah's prevalence over all creation, seen and unseen.

إِن يَنصُرْكُمُ ٱللَّهُ فَلَا غَالِبَ لَكُمْ ۖ وَإِن يَخْذُلْكُمْ
فَمَن ذَا ٱلَّذِى يَنصُرُكُم مِّنۢ بَعْدِهِۦ ۗ
وَعَلَى ٱللَّهِ فَلْيَتَوَكَّلِ ٱلْمُؤْمِنُونَ

160 If Allah assists you, then none can overcome you, and if He forsakes you, who is there that can assist besides Him? Upon Allah alone should the believers rely.

Allah will grant a person victory when he has followed the necessary rules, both the existing outer conditions and one's own inner state of strengths and weaknesses. When both the inner and outer are unified, we will experience success and see events in the light of truth. Then success is possible on all levels. If the path that we have taken is blocked, we must trust that a better path will be shown to us in time. We rely on good intention and correct effort, and act without being overly concerned with the outcome. Excess worry and concern will dissipate energy and can affect the outcome adversely.

وَمَا كَانَ لِنَبِيٍّ أَن يَغُلَّ ۚ وَمَن يَغْلُلْ يَأْتِ بِمَا غَلَّ يَوْمَ الْقِيَامَةِ ۚ
ثُمَّ تُوَفَّىٰ كُلُّ نَفْسٍ مَّا كَسَبَتْ وَهُمْ لَا يُظْلَمُونَ

161 And it is not proper that a prophet act dishonestly. Whoever acts dishonestly shall bear that dishonesty on the Day of Resurrection when every soul shall be repaid fully for what it has earned, and no one shall be dealt with unjustly.

The Prophet was accused by some hypocrites of hiding some cloth that had been captured in one of the battles. Here the Qur'an tells us that it is not possible for a prophet to act dishonestly. This verse describes hypocrisy and the way unfounded opinions and doubts slip into the mind. This verse refers specifically to the many people who were disturbed by the slander that was being spread. The answer to the believers as well as to us is that a man who has access to the Creator cannot betray the trust placed upon him. This is simply not possible.

Whoever betrays himself will see his betrayal on the Day of Reckoning, when there will be no injustice. In this life, we find apparent injustice, which is man's injustice, but in the next life this will not exist. The Qur'an also says that there are some people who accept the injustices that other men inflict upon them as though they were tests and afflictions from Allah. Surely, everything issues from Allah in the ultimate sense, but these people's direct cause of suffering is the injustice of other human beings, therefore they should not think that it is Allah punishing them. Allah does not punish those who do not bring punishment upon themselves. While recognizing the truth that, ultimately, everything comes from Allah, we must also realize that Allah has given us an intellect to escape from injustice or to put it right if possible. In the next experience, we will not suffer injustice, for divine justice will clearly prevail.

أَفَمَنِ اتَّبَعَ رِضْوَانَ اللَّهِ كَمَنْ بَآءَ بِسَخَطٍ مِّنَ اللَّهِ
وَمَأْوَيٰهُ جَهَنَّمُ وَبِئْسَ الْمَصِيرُ

162 Is then he who follows the pleasure of Allah like one who has made himself deserving of Allah's wrath? And his abode is Hell, a wretched destination.

One who follows 'the pleasure of Allah' finds contentment in his heart. How can it be the same for the one who acts correctly – in balance, in self-abandonment, and in knowledge – as it is for the one who blunders on in self-imposed ignorance? One man follows a certain direction with determination, while the other man shuts his eyes and acts haphazardly. The extent to which clarity and certainty rule the choice of a direction, together with the perseverance and patience with which that direction is followed, prove the follower's degree of faith and the state of unity (*tawḥīd*, تَوْحيد) that he possesses.

هُمْ دَرَجَاتٌ عِندَ اللَّهِ وَاللَّهُ بَصِيرٌ بِمَا يَعْمَلُونَ

163 There are degrees with Allah, and Allah sees what man does.

This verse explains that those who follow the pleasure of Allah do so in varying degrees, that is, there are degrees of faith, and there are degrees of translating faith accurately into action. Clearly, in this creation there is no equality at any level: no two prophets are the same; no two fingers are the same. However, there is justice and equity with Allah at all times. The greater the degree of faith, the more profound the true abandonment, and therefore the depth of knowledge and perception.

We cannot claim to have attained a certain degree of faith. The higher the degree of purification one attains, the more potential one has to move to even higher levels of subtle purification, and this correspondence unfolds infinitely. So long as there is breath in mān's breast, there is no resting place. That is one of the meanings of the prophetic tradition: 'There is no stopping place for the people of Medina.' Man cannot stop biologically, therefore, how can he stop spiritually? Because an echo of the Everlasting (*al-Ṣamad,* الصمد) exists in each one of us, we cannot stop the movement, change and unfolding of creation.

لَقَدْ مَنَّ ٱللَّهُ عَلَى ٱلْمُؤْمِنِينَ إِذْ بَعَثَ فِيهِمْ رَسُولًا مِنْ
أَنفُسِهِمْ يَتْلُوا۟ عَلَيْهِمْ ءَايَٰتِهِۦ وَيُزَكِّيهِمْ
وَيُعَلِّمُهُمُ ٱلْكِتَٰبَ وَٱلْحِكْمَةَ وَإِن كَانُوا۟ مِن قَبْلُ
لَفِى ضَلَٰلٍ مُّبِينٍ

164 Certainly, Allah bestowed a favour upon the believers when He brought forth from among them a Messenger, reciting His verses, purifying them, and teaching them the Book and wisdom, even though before that they were surely in manifest error.

A clear and direct favour was bestowed upon the people of Mecca who had not previously received a message or a messenger. 'A favour' demands a return. Allah rewards those who are in true faith: 'A reward never to be cut off' (95: 6).

'Reciting His verses ... teaching them the Book and wisdom': the Messenger repeatedly showed the Muslims both the inner and outer signs, such as the signs and reasons for their defeat at the Battle of Uḥud..

The Arabs were a people with a highly developed oral culture. Language was their highest art, and a person's level of culture was based on his knowledge of the language. The better one knew the language, the more esteem one had in the community. We can imagine the impact that the Prophet had upon his people when he brought a book which defied the best poets of his time to create anything comparable. The Qur'an predicts that at no time will anyone be able to produce any work of its quality. This in itself is one proof of its divine origin. As a result of this challenge and proof, the Messenger was able to convince the Arabs and show them the natural divine laws that governed existence. He was able to teach them the meaning of the Book, and show them Allah's decrees and that they had to obey and conform with those decrees in order to attain wisdom and perform correct actions, even though they had previously lived in a state of evident loss. In fact, they had been the most primitive, tribal and uncouth of people: family had been pitted against family and tribes had slain one another continuously.

أَوَلَمَّآ أَصَابَتْكُم مُّصِيبَةٌ قَدْ أَصَبْتُم مِّثْلَيْهَا قُلْتُمْ
أَنَّىٰ هَٰذَا ۖ قُلْ هُوَ مِنْ عِندِ أَنفُسِكُمْ ۗ
إِنَّ ٱللَّهَ عَلَىٰ كُلِّ شَيْءٍ قَدِيرٌ

165 **When a misfortune befell you, though you had afflicted them with twice as much, you began to say: How is this? Say: It is from yourselves. Surely, Allah has power over all things.**

Again this verse refers to the Battle of Uḥud. The sorrow and resultant reflection that the Muslims experienced is further described to us here. Although they suffered some losses, in the context of the overall conflict with the Meccan enemy, they were still way ahead, for at the Battle of Badr their victory was resounding, causing the Meccan forces the greatest dishonour.

When we think that we have sustained a loss, we must examine it in the larger context of our experience. We need to think of its meaning and value, and we should search ourselves to see what we have gained by the apparent loss. Man is at a loss because he measures events in a subjective and clumsy way. Here Allah reminds the Muslims that if they measure their losses correctly, they must take into account their victory at Badr and the victory of wisdom afforded to them by their loss at Uḥud..

To those who were dismayed at their defeat and asked in amazement why they had lost, the Qur'an answers, 'It is from yourselves.' The Qur'an thus implies that at Badr the Muslims were united; they acted as one band obedient to the Prophet. They were men of faith who did not fear death. At Uḥud., however, they lost the Badr spirit. At Uḥud., they listened to the voice of fear and divisiveness. The verse explains that it is the believer's responsibility to understand why they lost at Uḥud.

وَمَآ أَصَابَكُمْ يَوْمَ ٱلْتَقَى ٱلْجَمْعَانِ فَبِإِذْنِ ٱللَّهِ وَلِيَعْلَمَ ٱلْمُؤْمِنِينَ

166 What befell you on the day when the two armies met [at Uḥud] was by Allah's permission, that He might know the believers.

The two armies represent two opposing forces: faith and steadfastness against worldliness and disbelief. At every moment the battle between these two forces goes on in our hearts. That which befell the Muslims 'on the day when the two armies met' was contained in the knowledge of Allah and occurred by His permission. The meaning of the event is clear to those who have faith, who want to unveil the wiles of hypocrisy, to understand the meaning of trust, and to have the knowledge of unity.

وَلِيَعْلَمَ الَّذِينَ نَافَقُوا ۚ وَقِيلَ لَهُمْ تَعَالَوْا قَاتِلُوا فِي سَبِيلِ اللَّهِ
أَوِ ادْفَعُوا ۖ قَالُوا لَوْ نَعْلَمُ قِتَالًا لَاتَّبَعْنَاكُمْ ۗ هُمْ لِلْكُفْرِ
يَوْمَئِذٍ أَقْرَبُ مِنْهُمْ لِلْإِيمَانِ ۚ يَقُولُونَ بِأَفْوَاهِهِمْ مَا لَيْسَ فِي
قُلُوبِهِمْ ۗ وَاللَّهُ أَعْلَمُ بِمَا يَكْتُمُونَ

167 And that He might know the hypocrites. It was said to them: Come, fight in Allah's way, or defend your selves. They said: If we knew how to fight, we would certainly have followed you. They were, on that day, much nearer to unbelief than to belief. They say with their mouths what is not in their hearts. But Allah knows best what they conceal.

The hypocrites were those who, when told to fight in the way of Allah, said to the believers: 'If we had known how to fight we would have followed you.' 'Surely man is created with a hasty temperament, being greatly grieved when evil afflicts him, and niggardly when good befalls him' (70: 19-21). Man always seeks to understand the causes of any good that comes to him, but when affliction comes to him he blames others and makes excuses, refusing to look at the forces that brought about the affliction, and from which he might derive a lesson.

Allah says that these weak hearts are nearer to disbelief (*kufr*, كُفْر) than to belief (*īmān*, إِيمَان), indicating again that numerous degrees of belief exist. Life is given to us as a test, not to pass or fail, but to determine whether we are ready to penetrate further into the knowledge of truth. Allah holds back His knowledge from hearts that are not able to contain it. The more one's heart expands, the more it will receive that knowledge.

'They say with their mouths what is not in their hearts.' The Qur'an is about unity, and it guides us like children along the path of unification, so that we may unite our good intentions with correct actions. Without this inner unity, we are broken up in confusion. We keep one secret account of our lives only for ourselves, another .account for our companions, and a third account for the general public. Hypocrisy reflects a great inner confusion which will naturally cause sorrow and affliction. Until man unifies his inner being and becomes totally sincere, he is lost. Insincerity is the magnification of hypocrisy. 'And Allah knows best what they conceal.'

الَّذِينَ قَالُوا لِإِخْوَانِهِمْ وَقَعَدُوا لَوْ أَطَاعُونَا مَا قُتِلُوا
قُلْ فَادْرَءُوا عَنْ أَنفُسِكُمُ الْمَوْتَ
إِن كُنتُمْ صَادِقِينَ

168 Those who said of their brethren while they themselves held back: Had they obeyed us, they would not have been killed. Say: Then avert death if you speak the truth.

This verse confirms even more profoundly the message of verse 155, which concerned the uselessness of remorse. When the Muslims went back to Medina in misery over their defeat at Uḥud., they were met by those who had stayed back, and who had assumed the role of 'observers'. They said to the returning men that had the Prophet listened to their counsel, the undesirable outcome at Uḥud. would not have occurred. The Prophet, however, had no option but to fight, for the Meccans had come seeking revenge for Badr. He did not seek war; his reason for fighting was the defence of the young Muslim community. Originally, the Prophet had wished the Muslims to remain within the city and fight back from there, but the majority of the Muslims had wanted to come out of their homes and do battle.

Still fresh from their victory at Badr, they were over-confident. They also feared that remaining in the city could be construed as an act of cowardice.

In defiance the Qur'an says, 'Then avert death if you speak the truth.' Every aspect of life's events is within Allah's control. Reality is present, to teach us about Itself. We are not separate from the Divine Reality. The first lessons we are given by Reality concern our lower selves and the animal nature within us. The two symbols that are associated with the lower self are the dog and the pig. In ancient Egypt, the self is described as a chariot, in which rides the soul or priest drawn by a dog and a pig. The pig symbolizes desirous greed, and the dog symbolizes repulsion and aggression. Allah says that if they believe that the death of the Muslims could have been averted, then they should save themselves from death. How can anyone hope to stop destiny?

وَلَا تَحْسَبَنَّ الَّذِينَ قُتِلُوا فِي سَبِيلِ اللَّهِ أَمْوَاتًا ۚ
بَلْ أَحْيَاءٌ عِنْدَ رَبِّهِمْ يُرْزَقُونَ

169 Think not that those who are killed in Allah's way are dead. Rather, they are alive, provided with sustenance from their Lord.

فَرِحِينَ بِمَا آتَاهُمُ اللَّهُ مِنْ فَضْلِهِ وَيَسْتَبْشِرُونَ
بِالَّذِينَ لَمْ يَلْحَقُوا بِهِمْ مِنْ خَلْفِهِمْ
أَلَّا خَوْفٌ عَلَيْهِمْ وَلَا هُمْ يَحْزَنُونَ

170 Rejoicing in what Allah has given them from His bounty, and they rejoice for the sake of those who have not yet joined them, that they shall have no fear, nor shall they grieve.

'Those who are killed in Allah's way' are not dead, but alive in the state of spiritual consciousness, because they are martyrs or witnesses (*shuhada'*, شُهَداء) to the Truth. They remain in an intermediary realm, their spirits alive until the Day of Resurrection. Also, the memory of those who have died as martyrs is alive in perceptible ways, such as the people's love for them, and the attraction of others who wish to follow in their noble footsteps. The energy that they have generated through their act of sacrifice has an ongoing effect. Upon the face of the martyr (*shahīd*, شَهيد) as he dies in battle is a smile, and from his heart radiates pure joy. His soul experiences a state like that of the Garden.

'Rejoicing in what Allah has given them from His bounty'; Allah has given them the highest in consciousness and knowledge of Reality of which they had an experience in the physical realm. They rejoice over their final state of pure beingness and welcome others to join them. Their state is the prelude to the ultimate, final abode.

'They have no fear, nor shall they grieve.' Allah describes for us an intricate and perfectly balanced situation. 'Fear' (*khawf*, خَوف) refers especially to fear for the future. We fear that the future will not be conducive to our happiness, so we are usually preoccupied with insecurity and what the future will bring. 'Grief' (*ḥuzn*, حُزن) refers to the past. Allah implies by this phrase that those who are in the state of pure beingness look neither forward nor backward, for they are in the glorious, eternal present. They are in the presence of the Ever-living, the Self-Subsisting by Whom all things subsist (*al-Ḥayy al-Qayyūm*, الحَيّ القيّوم). They are not aware of something but are with awareness itself. They do not fear the future, because they are with the source and root of it.

When a person is fully aware, he trusts in his awareness. He is not afraid that he will lose it in the middle of his next action. Having neither fear nor sorrow means being present and available. This is the condition of the man of faith, a man who has given up everything, both past and future. A truly alert man with such a high consciousness cannot fail. Essentially, every person desires full awareness and wishes to avoid forgetfulness (*ghaflah*, غَفْلَة), because no one likes failure. We all wish to experience our destiny as had been decreed. Awareness based on faith illumines the decree.

يَسْتَبْشِرُونَ بِنِعْمَةٍ مِّنَ ٱللَّهِ وَفَضْلٍ
وَأَنَّ ٱللَّهَ لَا يُضِيعُ أَجْرَ ٱلْمُؤْمِنِينَ

171 They rejoice by Allah's favour and bounty, for Allah does not waste the reward of the believers.

They see nothing other than Allah's grace. Such is the true state of the believer. He sees his own faults at all times, while perceiving the constant mercy of Allah. This vision compels him to move on to higher degrees of consciousness and to strive for deeper perception and gnosis.

ٱلَّذِينَ ٱسْتَجَابُوا لِلَّهِ وَٱلرَّسُولِ مِنْ بَعْدِ مَآ أَصَابَهُمُ ٱلْقَرْحُ
لِلَّذِينَ أَحْسَنُوا مِنْهُمْ وَٱتَّقَوْا أَجْرٌ عَظِيمٌ

172 For those who responded to the call of Allah and the Messenger after they were wounded, do good, and guard themselves cautiously, there is a great reward.

The wound (*qarḥ*, قَرْح) was the result of the Muslims' misbehaviour at Uḥud. When we fail ourselves or those whom we hold in high esteem, we naturally feel regret. This regret is like a wound which, if encouraged to heal properly and not be reopened by a repetition of the same mistake, will render the injured person stronger than was before he suffered the wound.

الَّذِينَ قَالَ لَهُمُ النَّاسُ إِنَّ النَّاسَ قَدْ جَمَعُوا لَكُمْ فَاخْشَوْهُمْ
فَزَادَهُمْ إِيمَانًا وَقَالُوا حَسْبُنَا اللَّهُ وَنِعْمَ الْوَكِيلُ

173 Those to whom the people said: Surely, men have gathered against you, therefore, fear them; they were only increased in their faith, and they responded: Allah is sufficient for us and the Most Excellent Protector.

The story of Uḥud. never ends but is simply replayed in other places with different names and dates. After the Battle of Uḥud., Abu Sufyan gathered the Meccan army outside Medina for another battle. Reference is made here specifically to this event. Abu Sufyan had decided that it was time to eliminate the Muslims. At Uḥud. his army had only battered the Muslims but did not decisively win the war.

The spot where the Meccan army encamped was an established trading centre just outside Medina. The believers gathered around the Prophet were uncertain whether or not to go there to trade. The weaker among the Muslims tried to discourage the others by saying that people had gathered against them: 'Surely men have gathered against you, therefore fear them.' The believers responded by saying, 'Allah is sufficient for us and the Most Excellent Protector.'

فَانْقَلَبُوا بِنِعْمَةٍ مِنَ اللَّهِ وَفَضْلٍ لَمْ يَمْسَسْهُمْ سُوءٌ
وَاتَّبَعُوا رِضْوَانَ اللَّهِ ۗ وَاللَّهُ ذُو فَضْلٍ عَظِيمٍ

174 So they returned with favour from Allah and bounty. No misfortune touched them while they followed the pleasure of Allah, and Allah is the Possessor of Mighty Grace.

As a result of the Muslim's steadfastness, the enemy returned to Mecca. 'Favour from Allah' was a fear that entered the hearts of the enemy, and although they camped with Abu Sufyan only a few miles from Medina, they were undecided, hesitant and somewhat fearful of launching an attack. Consequently there was no battle and they returned to Mecca after some days, having eaten all of the food they had brought with them. The women of Mecca used to chide their men about this. Here Allah is encouraging the Muslims to carry on their business as best they can, and leave the rest to Allah, for if they speculate and calculate too much, they will become paralyzed.

'They followed the pleasure of Allah.' The pleasure of Allah is the pleasure of the believers. Allah wants nothing other than submission, contentment and correct action for the believer. This formula can only work if he walks the tightrope of 'the straight path' (*al-ṣirāṭ al-mustaqīm*, الصراط المُستَقيم), the path of awareness and knowledge. He gains admission to this path by displaying proper behaviour; that is, he must demonstrate fearlessness, compassion, correctness, willingness to turn to Allah for forgiveness, and willingness to abandon even his life in the cause of awakening to divine light.

إِنَّمَا ذَٰلِكُمُ الشَّيْطَٰنُ يُخَوِّفُ أَوْلِيَآءَهُۥ فَلَا تَخَافُوهُمْ
وَخَافُونِ إِن كُنتُم مُّؤْمِنِينَ

175 It is only Shayṭān that causes you to fear his friends, but do not fear them, fear Me, if you are believers.

In an earlier verse, the weaker Muslims cautioned the believers to fear the non-believers, but Allah says that 'It is only Shay ān that causes you to fear his friends.' In other words, the people who tried to discourage the Muslims were acting on the behest of the Shayṭān disguised as the voice of reason. More specifically, Shayṭān here refers to Abu Sufyan; traditional commentaries specify this point. Shaytan enters into the heart of man through the door of fear, by whispering to him that he will lose all that he is accustomed to, and will be destitute. He frightens only those who do not have an ideal to follow. Shayṭān gives up on those who will not be stopped by any obstacle on the path towards the knowledge of Allah.

'But do not fear them, fear Me.' Allah tells the believers not to be afraid of those who are the friends of the Shayṭān, for the believer is on the path of trust, and his only fear should be of transgressing the laws of Allah.

وَلَا يَحْزُنكَ الَّذِينَ يُسَارِعُونَ فِي الْكُفْرِ ۚ إِنَّهُمْ لَن يَضُرُّوا اللَّهَ
شَيْئًا ۗ يُرِيدُ اللَّهُ أَلَّا يَجْعَلَ لَهُمْ حَظًّا فِي الْآخِرَةِ ۖ
وَلَهُمْ عَذَابٌ عَظِيمٌ

176 Do not allow those who hasten to disbelief to cause you grief. Surely, they can do no harm at all to Allah. He intends not to give them any portion in the Hereafter, and they shall have a mighty chastisement.

The Qur'an tells us not to take as role models those who have amassed wealth and who seem to be strong. We must not be taken in by those who have deceived themselves regarding the true purpose in this life, nor should we pity them or let them bring us sorrow. The deniers may appear to be strong, but they are not: they clearly cause Allah no damage. Their apparent strength is the result of their temporary worldly power and arrogance. Allah has made the acquisition of the things of this world easy for them, and in relishing their wealth they have lost their hearts and the light within. Their hearts have become hard, and they will have no share of the next life. This fleeting existence is all they have.

The world is a garden for the non-believer (*kāfir*, كافِر) but a prison for the believer (*mu'min*, مُؤْمِن). Those who deny cause no harm to Allah, to the path of truth, or to the unfolding of this knowledge. They do not impede Allah in His decree, or in the purpose of His creation. They only deceive themselves. All they obtain is a short-lived, fleeting, dreamlike existence which quickly vanishes when their time is up.

إِنَّ الَّذِينَ اشْتَرَوُا الْكُفْرَ بِالْإِيمَانِ لَنْ يَضُرُّوا اللَّهَ
شَيْئًا ۖ وَلَهُمْ عَذَابٌ أَلِيمٌ

177 **Surely, those who have purchased disbelief at the price of faith shall do no harm at all to Allah, and they shall have a painful punishment.**

Again Allah emphasizes this extremely important point. They have exchanged their natural, innate potential to attain higher consciousness and gnosis through submission (*islām*, إسْلام) and faith (*īmān*, إيمان), for self-delusion and 'reasoned' disbelief (*kufr*, كُفر). They attract attention to themselves by claiming to be powerful and wealthy, and by pointing to their possessions, but they 'shall do no harm at all to Allah'. In truth, they will receive nothing other than torment (*'adhāb*, عَذاب) in this world and the next.

وَلَا يَحْسَبَنَّ الَّذِينَ كَفَرُوا أَنَّمَا نُمْلِي لَهُمْ خَيْرٌ لِأَنْفُسِهِمْ ۚ
إِنَّمَا نُمْلِي لَهُمْ لِيَزْدَادُوا إِثْمًا ۚ وَلَهُمْ عَذَابٌ مُهِينٌ

178 **And let not those who disbelieve think that Our granting them respite is good for them. We grant them respite only that they may add to their wrong actions, and they shall have a disgraceful chastisement.**

Allah does not give the non-believers increase in material possessions as a reward for their good deeds. Allah's generosity is such that He gives what is being asked. The people of this world are given their desires in this short-lived life only to be followed by regrets for ever.

'And they shall have a disgraceful chastisement.' Those who disbelieve will be degraded and will eventually experience disgrace in this world and the next. Look at the history of man to see how people fall into their own false securities and deceptions.

مَا كَانَ اللَّهُ لِيَذَرَ الْمُؤْمِنِينَ عَلَىٰ مَا أَنْتُمْ عَلَيْهِ حَتَّىٰ
يَمِيزَ الْخَبِيثَ مِنَ الطَّيِّبِ ۗ وَمَا كَانَ اللَّهُ لِيُطْلِعَكُمْ عَلَى
الْغَيْبِ وَلَٰكِنَّ اللَّهَ يَجْتَبِي مِنْ رُسُلِهِ مَنْ يَشَاءُ ۖ فَآمِنُوا بِاللَّهِ
وَرُسُلِهِ ۚ وَإِنْ تُؤْمِنُوا وَتَتَّقُوا فَلَكُمْ أَجْرٌ عَظِيمٌ

179 Allah will not leave the believers in the condition which you are in until He separates the evil from the good. Nor is Allah going to acquaint you with the Unseen, but Allah chooses His messengers as He pleases. Therefore, believe in Allah and His messengers. If you believe and guard yourselves cautiously, you shall obtain a great reward.

Those among the Muslims who are weak in faith or who are hypocritical are in that condition for their own ultimate good only if they take heed and become aware. How else may they recognize what is correct and what is not? How else may they move forward along the path of purification? The truth has nothing to do with the number of people who profess Islam and pray five times a day. These ritualistic acts can be performed without understanding their deeper inner meanings. But when the inner meaning is internalized, then the believer begins the process of transformation and awakening.

What must be learnt in life is correct discrimination: truth must be separated from falsehood, and hypocrisy revealed and eliminated. At all times, under whatever conditions, 'If you believe and guard cautiously, you shall have a great reward.' Trust in Allah is the first key to unlocking the door of truth. The heart of a person who trusts becomes calm, and a process of inner growth and higher consciousness is allowed to occur. Trust is an essential piece of armour protecting one from the uncertainty of the future. We have been told, 'Nor is Allah going to acquaint you with the Unseen.' We must accept our unknown futures and accept the present as it is, trusting in Allah's mercy and love for all creation.

وَلَا يَحْسَبَنَّ الَّذِينَ يَبْخَلُونَ بِمَا آتَاهُمُ اللَّهُ مِن فَضْلِهِ
هُوَ خَيْرًا لَّهُمْ بَلْ هُوَ شَرٌّ لَّهُمْ سَيُطَوَّقُونَ مَا بَخِلُوا بِهِ
يَوْمَ الْقِيَامَةِ وَلِلَّهِ مِيرَاثُ السَّمَاوَاتِ وَالْأَرْضِ
وَاللَّهُ بِمَا تَعْمَلُونَ خَبِيرٌ

180 And let not those who are miserly in giving that which Allah has granted them out of His grace, deem that it is good for them. Rather, it is worse for them. What they withheld shall be made to cling to their necks on the Day of Reckoning. To Allah belongs the legacy of the heavens and the earth, and Allah is aware of what you do.

We think that to keep and accumulate certain possessions for ourselves will give us security and happiness; but the cult of the self will eventually lead to destitution and barrenness. No positive end can come to those who hoard, for many of them will be crushed under the weight of their accumulation. The more belongings a person has that he is attached to, the more he groans under the millstone of anxiety and frantic insecurity.

'To Allah belongs the legacy of the heavens and earth.' A legacy (*mīrāth*, مِيراث), wealth or inheritance belongs to the one who has created it. All creation comes from Allah, is sustained by Allah and returns to Allah. Man is at best a guardian charged with the responsibility of disposing of Allah's gifts in the least harmful and most effective ways, without disturbing the balance and harmony of creation. If we cause imbalance, then we will ultimately afflict ourselves or the generations after us with the unwelcome result.

لَقَدْ سَمِعَ اللَّهُ قَوْلَ الَّذِينَ قَالُوا إِنَّ اللَّهَ فَقِيرٌ وَنَحْنُ
أَغْنِيَاءُ سَنَكْتُبُ مَا قَالُوا وَقَتْلَهُمُ الْأَنْبِيَاءَ بِغَيْرِ
حَقٍّ وَنَقُولُ ذُوقُوا عَذَابَ الْحَرِيقِ

181 **Allah has certainly heard the saying of those who said: Surely, Allah is poor, and we are rich. We will record what they say and their killing the prophets unjustly. We will say: Taste the chastisement of burning.**

ذَٰلِكَ بِمَا قَدَّمَتْ أَيْدِيكُمْ وَأَنَّ اللَّهَ لَيْسَ بِظَلَّامٍ لِلْعَبِيدِ

182 **This is for what your own hands have sent forth, and Allah is not in the least unjust to mankind.**

When the verse 'Who will offer to Allah a goodly loan that He may double it for him' (57: 11) was revealed, the money-lenders said, 'Surely, Allah is poor, and we are rich.' Their intellects were so shallow that everything they thought about could only be understood in the context of material wealth and money.

Man's perpetual preoccupation in dealing with the material world and his desire for acquisitions is a tragic flaw in his character that needs to be remedied by accepting Allah's lordship and dedicating some effort towards divine knowledge.

'We will record what they say.' What they say is written upon them, and is proof of the state of their ignorance. The Jews, who killed many of the prophets who came to them, will experience 'the chastisement of burning'.

الَّذِينَ قَالُوا إِنَّ اللَّهَ عَهِدَ إِلَيْنَا أَلَّا نُؤْمِنَ
لِرَسُولٍ حَتَّىٰ يَأْتِيَنَا بِقُرْبَانٍ تَأْكُلُهُ النَّارُ قُلْ
قَدْ جَاءَكُمْ رُسُلٌ مِنْ قَبْلِي بِالْبَيِّنَاتِ وَبِالَّذِي قُلْتُمْ
فَلِمَ قَتَلْتُمُوهُمْ إِنْ كُنْتُمْ صَادِقِينَ

183 **Those who said: Surely, Allah has enjoined upon us that we should not believe in any messenger until he brings us an offering which the fire consumes. Say: Indeed, messengers came to you before me with clear arguments [i.e. reasoning] and with that which you mentioned. Why then did you kill them if you are truthful?**

The Jews claimed that they were enjoined by Allah not to believe in any messenger until there was a miraculous sign. They do not want to see that the Prophet and the Qur'an were indeed the clear signs. They required that the awaited sign be a physical manifestation foretold (supposedly) in their scriptures. Allah tells the Prophet to remind them that many signs have already come to them which met their demands, and that many prophets had also come to them in the past, but were killed unjustly. A person who seeks to deny will always find justification. Shāyṭan's ways have unending permutations.

فَإِن كَذَّبُوكَ فَقَدْ كُذِّبَ رُسُلٌ مِّن قَبْلِكَ
جَآءُو بِالْبَيِّنَاتِ وَالزُّبُرِ وَالْكِتَابِ الْمُنِيرِ

184 So if they reject you, indeed, before you were other messengers who were also rejected. They came with clear proofs, scriptures, and the illuminating book.

Allah informs the Prophet that man's lower nature is to deny the truth which is undesirable. 'Surely man is in loss' (103: 2). Loss is his condition as long as he does not learn from the blessedness of afflictions and tests which are, in fact, urging him to act differently. The correct action is that which is in harmony with Allah's decree and purpose of creation.

كُلُّ نَفْسٍ ذَآئِقَةُ الْمَوْتِ ۗ وَإِنَّمَا تُوَفَّوْنَ
أُجُورَكُمْ يَوْمَ الْقِيَامَةِ ۖ فَمَن زُحْزِحَ عَنِ النَّارِ
وَأُدْخِلَ الْجَنَّةَ فَقَدْ فَازَ ۗ وَمَا الْحَيَوٰةُ
الدُّنْيَآ إِلَّا مَتَاعُ الْغُرُورِ

185 Every soul shall taste death, and you shall be repaid fully on the Resurrection Day. Whoever is then removed far from the Fire and is caused to enter the Garden has indeed triumphed. And the life of this world is nothing but deceptive pleasure.

There is no escape from the taste of death. Why should one fear the inevitable unless there is something wrong with one's direction and understanding? The human body is destined to be left behind on earth, through a process called death. The soul is to journey onwards in the Unseen.

'Whoever is removed far from the Fire': it is as though man is standing at the edge of the Fire. Man must be shaken in order to cease dwelling in his lower, lethargic nature. He must be shaken free from the grip of his false imagination and then be directed towards the Garden of inner meanings. Whoever is shaken 'has indeed triumphed', for 'the life of this world is nothing but deceptive pleasure'. It is deceptive because it is short-lived and is a prelude to the real life, everlasting, and free of time and space.

لَتُبْلَوُنَّ فِيٓ أَمْوَٰلِكُمْ وَأَنفُسِكُمْ وَلَتَسْمَعُنَّ
مِنَ ٱلَّذِينَ أُوتُوا ٱلْكِتَٰبَ مِن قَبْلِكُمْ وَمِنَ ٱلَّذِينَ
أَشْرَكُوٓا أَذًى كَثِيرًا ۚ وَإِن تَصْبِرُوا وَتَتَّقُوا
فَإِنَّ ذَٰلِكَ مِنْ عَزْمِ ٱلْأُمُورِ

186 You shall certainly be tried in regard to your wealth and your souls, and you shall certainly hear annoying things from those who have been given the Book before you and from those who associate with Allah. If you are patient and guard yourselves cautiously, surely, this is of the most resolute affairs.

There is no way to avoid being tested, tried and afflicted. This life is the melting – pot wherein we learn (or refuse to learn) about following the path of faith and submission named Islam. Allah says that human beings will be afflicted in their wealth and possessions, and within themselves. It is the nature of the one who trusts in Allah to be strengthened by outer difficulties and affliction. The more he is tested and tried, the more he learns and recognizes his dependence on Allah. None but Allah offers him a reliable refuge.

The person of faith and submission is fully involved in the mundane life of a community, yet he remains inwardly separate from creation, experiencing closeness, dependence and love for Allah. He knows that every human being has the potential to possess knowledge, understanding and compassion, but he sees that most people waste their potential. This vision is a great affliction upon him as well as a driving force to serve, guide and assist in the way of Allah.

وَإِذْ أَخَذَ ٱللَّهُ مِيثَٰقَ ٱلَّذِينَ أُوتُوا۟ ٱلْكِتَٰبَ لَتُبَيِّنُنَّهُۥ
لِلنَّاسِ وَلَا تَكْتُمُونَهُۥ فَنَبَذُوهُ وَرَآءَ ظُهُورِهِمْ
وَٱشْتَرَوْا۟ بِهِۦ ثَمَنًا قَلِيلًا ۖ فَبِئْسَ مَا يَشْتَرُونَ

187 And when Allah made a covenant with those who were given the Book: You shall explain it to men and you shall not conceal it. But they cast it behind their backs and exchanged it for a small price. How wretched and inconsequential is that which they buy.

When a people has been blessed with a prophetic message, it is incumbent upon them to live according to its truth. If, after having been given the true path, they exchange it for something transient and lowly, then 'wretched and inconsequential is that which they buy'. They could not do worse: the opportunity to evolve fully and awaken to the inner light has been lost.

لَا تَحْسَبَنَّ ٱلَّذِينَ يَفْرَحُونَ بِمَآ أَتَوا۟ وَّيُحِبُّونَ
أَن يُحْمَدُوا۟ بِمَا لَمْ يَفْعَلُوا۟ فَلَا تَحْسَبَنَّهُم بِمَفَازَةٍ
مِّنَ ٱلْعَذَابِ ۖ وَلَهُمْ عَذَابٌ أَلِيمٌ

188 Do not think that those who exult in what they have

accomplished, and love to be praised for what they have not accomplished, are safe from chastisement. They shall have a painful punishment.

The Qur'an gives us an amazing insight into man's nature. Reality exposes our weaknesses, so that we are led to the realization of unity, and unification with the Truth – and thereby inner freedom and outer contentment.

وَلِلَّهِ مُلْكُ السَّمَاوَاتِ وَالْأَرْضِ ۗ وَاللَّهُ
عَلَىٰ كُلِّ شَيْءٍ قَدِيرٌ

189 To Allah belongs the kingdom of the heavens and the earth, and Allah has power over all things.

There is no escape from the power of Allah, neither in this life nor in the next. Allah's power permeates the Seen and Unseen worlds.

إِنَّ فِي خَلْقِ السَّمَاوَاتِ وَالْأَرْضِ وَاخْتِلَافِ اللَّيْلِ
وَالنَّهَارِ لَآيَاتٍ لِأُولِي الْأَلْبَابِ

190 In the creation of the heavens and the earth, and the alternation of night and day, are signs for men of deep understanding.

These last verses of the chapter clearly delineate the true path of belief in Allah. What is the way to the ultimate truth? What is the way towards salvation upon the Ark of Noah? How do we become truly abandoned in Allah and recognize the abundant reward here and now? We can start by reflecting upon the statement, 'In the creation of the heavens and the earth ... are signs for men of deep understanding.' If we look at the phenomenon of day and night and observe how one blends into the other, we see, in fact, that each causes the other. In a like manner, ignorance dies and begets knowledge, dependence on other than Allah dies and dependence on Allah is born. 'He brings forth the living from the dead and the dead from the living' (10: 31). We have the ability to discern which direction we must take: one direction leads to a dead end, and the other leads to expansion and inner freedom.

الَّذِينَ يَذْكُرُونَ اللَّهَ قِيَامًا وَقُعُودًا وَعَلَىٰ جُنُوبِهِمْ
وَيَتَفَكَّرُونَ فِي خَلْقِ السَّمَاوَاتِ وَالْأَرْضِ رَبَّنَا
مَا خَلَقْتَ هَٰذَا بَاطِلًا سُبْحَانَكَ فَقِنَا عَذَابَ النَّارِ

191 **Those who remember Allah while standing, sitting, and lying on their sides, and who reflect on the creation of the heavens and the earth: Our Lord, You have not created this in vain! Glory be to You! Save us, then, from the chastisement of the Fire.**

This verse defines the men of deep understanding and of sound heart (*ulū al-albāb,* أولوُ الألْبَاب), those who remember and see in these changes, in these dualities, nothing other than the signs of One God. They remember Him while standing, sitting and lying down. At all times they are in a state of prayer, praise, gratitude and spontaneous awareness.

'And who reflect upon the creation of the heavens and the earth': there is a Prophetic tradition which says, 'The reflection of an hour is better than the [formal] worship of seventy years.' Another tradition substitutes one year for seventy, and other variations on the same theme also exist. The point is that our worship must be real, sincere and transformative. It must issue from our innermost core. If we do not attain to this state of worship, our acts are but the outer shells of worship. The inner kernel is what gives nourishment. Participating in the form alone, however, is necessary, and it is better than not worshipping at all, for 'there are degrees with Allah'. We must accept all those who profess Islam as our brothers, for Allah's mercy is upon all creation, even the man who simply goes through the ritualistic motions of prayer.

People of deep understanding worship, reflect and remember within the deepest recesses of their heart. In order to arrive at this state, the veils of self-deception and ego in man have to be deconstructed and removed. This is a difficult task. Each person must unveil himself by reflecting upon the truth: that this creation, which is manifested as apparent duality, is in fact permeated by unity. No cause and effect can exist without a first original cause, the same cause that brought all of creation into beingness. Thus, the task is to discover our own source. To do this one must determine the exact direction to follow, reduce the quantity of one's thoughts and improve their quality, purify one's intentions and heart, and finally unify one's intentions with appropriate actions: inner delight and light balanced by outer discipline and clear direction.

In searching for the cause of one's existence, one eventually discovers that Allah's creation was produced for Allah's pleasure. He creates without question, but man is to be questioned. Man must come to realize that the answer to the question of his existence emanates from the very source from which the question arises. Allah gives us the power and faculty to question and He also guides us to the answer by exclusion. The answer is that there is no god except God.

رَبَّنَآ إِنَّكَ مَن تُدْخِلِ ٱلنَّارَ فَقَدْ أَخْزَيْتَهُۥ ۖ
وَمَا لِلظَّٰلِمِينَ مِنْ أَنصَارٍ

192 Our Lord, whomever You cause to enter the Fire has indeed been brought to disgrace. There shall be no helpers for the unjust.

The life of the one referred to in this verse is disgracefully wasted, beyond hope of amendment, because it has already been squandered. The Qur'an says that he who is in the Fire has been shamed, meaning that he has wrongfully expended his energy and time.

رَبَّنَآ إِنَّنَا سَمِعْنَا مُنَادِيًا يُنَادِي لِلْإِيمَانِ أَنْ ءَامِنُوا۟ بِرَبِّكُمْ فَـَٔامَنَّا ۚ
رَبَّنَا فَٱغْفِرْ لَنَا ذُنُوبَنَا وَكَفِّرْ عَنَّا سَيِّـَٔاتِنَا وَتَوَفَّنَا مَعَ ٱلْأَبْرَارِ

193 Our Lord, surely we have heard a crier calling to the faith, saying: Believe in your Lord, so we believed. Our Lord, forgive our faults, cover our wrong actions, and cause us to die among the righteous.

Surely we have heard the inner calling to the truth, and we have recognized it in our hearts. This was the message of the Prophet Muhammad. 'And from the remote part of the city there came a man running. He said, "O my people, follow the messengers. Follow those who do not ask you for any reward and are guided" (36: 20). People who are wholesome, sound, contained and sensitive will hear the voice of the truth and will discriminate. These are the people who recognize and read the Book. They heard the call instructing them to trust in their Creator, to recognize the limits of their freedom, and not to transgress. For those who are within the sanctuary of Islam, all is well in this world and the next. The voice calls, asking us to recognize our humanity, and to trust in the Lordship which fulfils each of us, in order to take us to our full potential. We mature by accepting and dealing with the problems and changes that are placed in front of us. It is through interaction that we are guided towards an ever-narrowing field of action, until finally we find that there is no escape except through submission and correct action. All apparent dualities are contained in the oneness of purpose and the unique source of all creation.

'Our Lord ... cause us to die among the righteous.' The righteous (*abrār*, أَبْرَار) are people who possess qualities of inner reverence, piety, devoutness and kindness. They are striving towards their perfection. They ask Allah to forgive and heal them for having remained negligent in any way after the signs had come to them.

رَبَّنَا وَءَاتِنَا مَا وَعَدتَّنَا عَلَىٰ رُسُلِكَ وَلَا تُخْزِنَا
يَوْمَ الْقِيَٰمَةِ إِنَّكَ لَا تُخْلِفُ الْمِيعَادَ

194 Our Lord, grant us what You have promised us by Your messengers, and disgrace us not on the Day of Reckoning. Surely, You do not fail to perform [Your] promises.

This is the song which issues from the heart of the believer as he progresses along the path of enlightenment. He seeks complete freedom through submission to Lordship (*rubūbīyyah,* رُبُوبِيَّة). He is calling upon the Lord, thus showing his desire to progress towards his fully developed potential, the state of gnosis.

'Grant us what You have promised us by Your messengers.' At first his trust is more of a blind faith in the outward form of the message. He trusts that it is the true message, brought by a man of Allah, one who is living the message transformed by it, and who is not afraid of any consequences that might result from his belief or actions. The believer asks that, since he has trusted in the message, he not be disgraced on the Day of Resurrection. His plea shows his yearning for divine guidance and protection. That in which he believes becomes a reality. If one fails to achieve this goal, then it is simply because one has not followed the path of submission, knowledge, action and thereby transformation.

فَاسْتَجَابَ لَهُمْ رَبُّهُمْ أَنِّي لَا أُضِيعُ عَمَلَ عَامِلٍ مِّنكُم مِّن ذَكَرٍ
أَوْ أُنثَىٰ ۖ بَعْضُكُم مِّن بَعْضٍ ۖ فَالَّذِينَ هَاجَرُوا وَأُخْرِجُوا مِن
دِيَارِهِمْ وَأُوذُوا فِي سَبِيلِي وَقَاتَلُوا وَقُتِلُوا لَأُكَفِّرَنَّ عَنْهُمْ
سَيِّئَاتِهِمْ وَلَأُدْخِلَنَّهُمْ جَنَّاتٍ تَجْرِي مِن تَحْتِهَا الْأَنْهَارُ
ثَوَابًا مِّنْ عِندِ اللَّهِ ۗ وَاللَّهُ عِندَهُ حُسْنُ الثَّوَابِ

195 **So their Lord heard their prayer [and said]: I will not waste the work of any one among you, whether male or female, the one of you being from the other. Those who fled, who were turned out of their homes, who were persecuted in My way, and who fought and were slain, I will most certainly forgive their wrong actions and cause them to enter gardens beneath which rivers flow – a reward from Allah. And with Allah is the best reward.**

The generous Lord has obligated Himself to answer one's prayers. This is a law of existence. The man of faith will see that this is true according to the degree of his faith. When one is not frightened of the future, one is able to see into it more clearly, that is, to the extent that the mercy of Allah does not hide what is coming. Accepting the will of Allah allows one to act positively and with clarity of purpose. At a certain point in one's evolvement one enters into a timeless realm in which the future, a concept which is trapped within time, ceases to have the usual meaning. Only those with the strongest faith, such as the prophets and great men of Allah, are in the fulfilling state of beingness and pure consciousness. The specific knowledge of future events is only given in accordance with one's ability to handle it. To give this gift to a weak man would be like giving a young untrained boy a gun. It contains too much power to risk putting it into the wrong hands: this is not the way of Reality. Knowledge of the future is a gift from Allah. A glimpse of the future may be a part of the small confirmations that the weaker believer receives; such glimpses are not miracles. The true miracle is creation itself, including each one of us. The miracle is that from one source a multitude has emanated and all will return back to that source.

'I will not waste the work'; Allah's justice is absolute. It is man who is unjust, through ignorance. A person who is constantly chasing after elusive desires will ultimately lose. He will find that time has passed and no higher awakening and fulfilment has been attained. A person whose intention is to value every moment of life and use it to develop his full potential will be ready to receive the gifts which Allah bestows, all according to Allah's timing.

'Those who fled, who were turned out of their homes ... and who fought and were slain': the basic rule is that a Muslim fights only in self-defence. 'They killed and were killed', means that they responded. Their wrong actions were obliterated because of their faith in Allah, correct actions and self-sacrifice.

'Gardens beneath which rivers flow – a reward from Allah. And with Allah is the best reward.' This is the ultimate, timeless, spaceless Garden. In this world there are the outer gardens as well as the gardens of knowledge, obedience and gratitude, whose rivers are inward and thus unseen. These gardens have their own intrinsic reward, and are thus fed from an unseen source. Inner bliss has no outer reason.

لَا يَغُرَّنَّكَ تَقَلُّبُ الَّذِينَ كَفَرُوا فِي الْبِلَادِ

196 Let it not deceive you that those who disbelieve go to and fro in the cities freely.

مَتَاعٌ قَلِيلٌ ثُمَّ مَأْوَاهُمْ جَهَنَّمُ وَبِئْسَ الْمِهَادُ

197 A brief enjoyment, then their abode is Hell: a miserable place of rest.

Do not be deceived by the apparent freedom of those who have high social status or great wealth. Theirs is 'a brief enjoyment', which they have purchased at an exorbitantly high price, for the consequence of this mindless fling is the Fire, an unalterable and eternal state.

لَٰكِنِ الَّذِينَ اتَّقَوْا رَبَّهُمْ لَهُمْ جَنَّاتٌ تَجْرِي مِن تَحْتِهَا
الْأَنْهَارُ خَالِدِينَ فِيهَا نُزُلًا مِّنْ عِندِ
اللَّهِ وَمَا عِندَ اللَّهِ خَيْرٌ لِّلْأَبْرَارِ

198 But those who guard themselves carefully shall have gardens beneath which rivers flow, abiding in them forever: a dwelling place from their Lord. And what is with Allah is best for the righteous.

The Qur'an constantly sets forth discriminative situations for us in order to awaken our intellects. We are told of physical events, such as battles between opposing forces. Then the Qur'an goes deeper into more subtle descriptions. We are shown the entire spectrum of belief. The Qur'an is made of one fibre, whose many strands are interwoven. The more closely we examine it, the finer is the wholesomeness as well as the distinctions we find. It is an unending sea of knowledge, light and delight.

In this chapter we are given examples of those who are drowned in disbelief, those who are less engulfed, as well as those who are strong in faith, and those who are weaker. We are also shown how hypocrisy springs up during moments when we have been overcome by a false sense of security and self-confidence, and how this very hypocrisy, if it is clearly recognized, may help to increase our awareness. The Qur'an then presents to us the portrait of the righteous, those who are cautious of their Lord. They are in perpetual, fearful awareness and have high expectations spiritually. Their awareness and remembrance is intrinsically rewarded with inward gardens of delightful understanding and love for Allah.

وَإِنَّ مِنْ أَهْلِ الْكِتَابِ لَمَن يُؤْمِنُ بِاللَّهِ وَمَا أُنزِلَ إِلَيْكُمْ
وَمَا أُنزِلَ إِلَيْهِمْ خَاشِعِينَ لِلَّهِ لَا يَشْتَرُونَ بِآيَاتِ
اللَّهِ ثَمَنًا قَلِيلًا أُولَٰئِكَ لَهُمْ أَجْرُهُمْ عِندَ
رَبِّهِمْ إِنَّ اللَّهَ سَرِيعُ الْحِسَابِ

199 And surely among the People of the Book are those who believe in Allah, and [in] that which has been revealed to you and to them. They are humble before Allah and do not exchange the communications of Allah for a trifling price. They have their reward with their Lord. Surely, Allah is quick to take account.

Those who are truly People of the Book, particularly the genuine and committed Jews and Christians, will naturally believe in the Qur'an, because they know that there is only one Book sent by Allah. They will believe in the unity and perfection of Allah's message, which combines the outer Law and the inner realization of Reality. We are reminded not to consider all the People of the Book as deniers simply because their books have been changed or abrogated. There are among them people who are truly in a state of abandonment to Allah. They believe in Allah and live in true submission and obedience. They will not exchange their belief for anything of this world. Obviously, such people are the minority. The Qur'an demonstrates the respect that Islam accords the People of the Book, for all the previous prophets and messengers were prophets of Allah's one religion - Islam. We must not become arrogant simply because we think we are followers of Muhammad, for how many Muslims really do follow him?

يَٰٓأَيُّهَا ٱلَّذِينَ ءَامَنُوا۟ ٱصْبِرُوا۟ وَصَابِرُوا۟ وَرَابِطُوا۟
وَٱتَّقُوا۟ ٱللَّهَ لَعَلَّكُمْ تُفْلِحُونَ

200 O you who believe, be patient and excel in patience; remain steadfast and [guard yourselves], and keep your duty to Allah that you may be successful.

A true believer is patient with whatever afflicts him. He is patient because he believes in Allah's wisdom and mercy and that he will come to know the benefit of his problems and their meaning: learning through experience. He is patient in living without what is forbidden to him. He is patient during hardship, in the knowledge that all is well at the end. Allah exhorts him to win over his enemy: his ego-self, the arch-enemy of living according to unity (*tawḥīd* ، تَوْحيد).

We can only help others to experience spirituality and to progress along the path as long as there is an environment that is conducive to such experiences. Only very few of the strong believers can survive in isolation, in the middle of an exploitative, materialistic and competitive culture. Such an environment may strengthen those who are already strong, but will certainly cause much trouble and confusion for the weak in faith. The majority of us need the reinforcement of those who are like-minded; safety and security is not to be found in numbers alone, but in the quality of those who make up the community of believers.

'And guard yourselves carefully before Allah that you may be successful.' If we stay within the bounds set by Allah, outwardly as well as inwardly, we ourselves will recognize the bounds of what is permitted and what is forbidden. We must learn the extent of our faith in order to apply the right remedies to our inner maladies. A weak person must follow those who are strong. It is for this reason that those who are on the path of knowledge join other like-minded souls wherever they are, always looking to stronger believers for guidance.

Those who do not join the community of believers mistakenly presume that they can attain knowledge of truth and unity by isolation. We must remember, however, that the strength of a community is not in its size. The Prophet Muhammad said, 'It is better to bring one heart to the knowledge of the truth than to own everything in the heaven or earth.'

There is no higher reward for an enlightened being in this existence than seeing others progress in self-knowledge and gnosis. Though a man's spiritual aspirations may be buried under the debris of his lower self, this debris can be removed and the individual uplifted and improved when the environment exists in which he is given inner health, strength and guidance. Difficulties must be tackled correctly and efficiently, with a sensitivity to the learning process that lies therein. One calls upon Allah with sincerity and humility for understanding and guidance.

SUMMARY

The message of the Chapter of The Family of 'Imrān is the message of the Qur'an. This message is based on Unity, the Oneness of Allah: 'Allah, there is no god but Him, the Living, the Self-Subsisting... nothing in the earth or heavens is hidden from Allah...He fashions you in the womb as He pleases. There is no god except Him ... the Almighty, the Wise ... Sovereign Master of the kingdom ... the Forgiving, the Merciful.'

The Family of 'Imrān, like the rest of the Qur'an, moves back and forth between essential statements about the nature of Reality and the psycho-social condition of man. Upon reflection, one will notice that in a sense it copies the nature of man's consciousness which also moves back and forth, from lesser or greater introspection to lesser or greater degrees of social involvement, though everyone is both inwardly and outwardly involved at all times. Even in times of complete physical isolation, deeply engrossed in a meditative state, one's physical body is still interacting with the environment. And even in times of the most active social involvement, one is still connected to one's inward subtle processes. The inward and the outward are but two sides of one being.

Unity (*tawḥīd*, تَوْحِيد) relates to pure consciousness and unified beingness. There is no way to attain such a state except by believing in it and by continuous struggle with good actions. For this reason, the Book is important as a technical manual of guidance. Through belief and purification comes the experiential certainty that 'there is no god but He'. As simple as the path to this ultimate state seems, the attractiveness of the world is a lure which continually diverts man's attention: 'Alluring for mankind is the desirous love of women, offspring, stored-up treasure of gold and silver ... that is the pleasure of the life of the world.' The only way for him to avoid its snares is by patiently guarding his heart, examining his intentions with scrupulous honesty, and turning again and again to Allah: ' They said, Our Lord, forgive us for our wrong actions and extravagance ... and help us against those who disbelieve.'

In The Family of 'Imrān, Allah has described the various levels and degrees of faith which exist among mankind, as well as the changes which take place within the heart of the one who possesses faith. The heart is never fixed or stationary. Fixation only occurs in the realm outside time, and ultimate certainty is only achieved through death, when one no longer has any freedom to act. The closer one is to the point of death, the more one is likely to become certain of Reality.

What, then, does faith (*īmān*, إيمان) mean? Can it be translated into knowledge, or is it just a kind of superstitious belief? Faith may begin blindly, but if it does not lead to truly awakened belief, then it has very little value. Faith is only as strong as the connection between the believer and the One in Whom he believes and trusts. Faith and trust open up the door to knowledge and correct actions. With these elements as foundation stones, transformation can begin.

One cannot be connected to Allah unless one is also connected to Him through His creation, for where is it that Allah is not? A person who claims to be connected only with Allah and not His creation is insincere or ignorant, because such a statement implies separation, and there is none, as Allah says, 'We are nearer to him than his jugular vein' (50: 16).

Faith in Allah purifies the believer. True Islam is based on the purity of hearts. What is the degree of their abandonment, freedom and availability? Do hearts yearn for the things of this world while they are unable to obtain them? The heart reflects the degree of knowledge and unity. Faith is increased by the practice of guarding oneself carefully before Allah, for one realizes that this is necessary.

It is impossible for one to judge whether someone has acted out of faith or not, because one does not know the changes that another's heart has undergone. All that can be said is that a person's actions at a particular moment are a reflection of his inner state, be it one of weakness, confusion and hate, or strength, direction and love. A person's actions are the reflection of a moment and may very well be different in the future. Criticism should be made only of a person's actions and not of the person himself, because these actions stem from intentions which may be good or bad.

Though the central action in The Family of 'Imrān is the Battle of Uḥud, the chapter also contains the essential Qur'anic narrative about the Prophet Jesus. Most of this narrative describes the miraculous circumstances of his birth, and the miracles which he wrought to jolt the people who had been mesmerized by an elite rabbinical group.

The Battle of Uḥud had a shock effect upon the young Muslim community, which had become over-confident after their stunning victory at Badr. The loss to the Meccan force, headed by Abu Sufyan, provided the motive for the revelation of many verses which gave subtle indications and knowledge about the battle of the higher and lower aspects of man's self. In Arabic the term for this battle is *jihād* (جهاد). Now *jihād* is usually translated as 'holy war', but it actually means 'struggle in the way of truth'. The Prophet Muhammad explained that the physical battle in defense of the truth is the minor *jihād*. The major *jihād*, he said, was the struggle against the lower self. Thus, enclosed within the verses dealing with the Battle of Uḥud is direct knowledge about the battle against the lower self.

From the Qur'an's instruction about the self in The Family of 'Imrān we can grasp the meaning of the verse, 'Certainly the self bids to trouble' (12: 53). We come to understand the self more deeply, as the locus of human experience, in its dual capacity for good and evil. In our time, particularly in the world culture of techno-usury, the fog of 'civilized' illusion is thick. Many people recognize the ills, but few see the remedies. Even though unsullied goodness is rarely seen, so many personifications of evil have passed across the world stage that logic dictates the necessity for the emergence of a higher level of the self. If this were not the case, humanity would no longer exist, for the side of the scale against life would have tipped over long ago.

'The signs of Allah that We recite to you in truth' are continually flashing before us, but if we cannot stand the light of truth, then we are blinded by the after-images of worldly existence, and we merely grope about without direction. Stunned by the demands and desires of the lower self, unable to transform them by a higher degree of awareness, we completely miss the greatest miracle of all: existence itself. Our stale perception, however, constantly clouds this wondrous, continuously unfolding miracle: 'They have hearts that do not understand and eyes that do not perceive' (7: 179).

Hypocrisy (*nifāq*, نِفاق) is the key malady, because it is the one which the ego-self (*nafs*, نَفْس) relishes. In hypocrisy, the lower self finds an excuse and an escape; the hypocrite hides in the tunnel of his own fabrication. Hypocrisy is very elusive and difficult to trap at the source. Even some of the best among the believers were afflicted by hypocrisy in the Battle of Uḥud. We must never consider ourselves above others. 'None feel secure from Allah's plan except the people who are at a loss' (7: 99). Allah's plan and decree is to awaken us to Allah.

Reality tests and afflicts us in order to purify and awaken us. During the most difficult times we have indeed the best opportunity to reflect upon the reasons why conflicts occur. During ordinary and uneventful times habits are in control, and little knowledge is gained. During times of trouble and change, however, we are forced to submit, and from that submission we learn the meaning behind events and gain wisdom and subtle knowledge.

The Family of 'Imrān is a more detailed description of the events recounted in the chapter The Time (*Al-'Aṣr*, العصر). 'Throughout time, man is at a loss, except those who believe, act correctly, exhort to truth and exhort to patience' (103: 1-3). The key theme is man's hypocrisy and confusion. An object can be seen most clearly when it has sharply defined shadows; that which is transparent is not seen at all in dim light. The greater the shadow, the more obvious the profile. The shadow of hypocrisy loomed long and large across the scene of events in the early days of Islam, and could therefore be spotted by the believers.

The subtle hypocrisies that we harbour were present in the early community of Medina. Just as those who doubted and did not manifest true trust in Allah existed in the early community, so they exist within the communities of Muslims today. The way of Allah does not change. If it were to change, there would be chaos and constant disruption in creation. If it were to change, there would be no relationship or continuity between past, present and future.

The Family of 'Imrān describes the central pivot upon which Islam, civilization, culture and humanity in general rest: the community of believers in Allah. The worth of a community can be judged by its objective and orientation. The primary desire and goal of the first Muslim community was the knowledge of unity. The community of early Islam in Medina not only experienced the knowledge of unity, but lived it; and many were transformed by it. They were 'unifiers' (*muwaḥḥidīn*, مُوَحِدين) in the true sense. They believed that the source of the entire creation is One and that the whole of creation is sustained by, and reverts back to, the One Lord. They recognized the Attributes of Allah as they were manifested in the realm of experiential reality.

After their faith and understanding of the oneness of Reality, the second force which connected the Muslims of Medina was their trust in the Prophet Muhammad and their love and loyalty to him. By their love and faith in Allah, inner transformation occurred. By love of, and obedience to, the prophetic teaching, the community and society of believers emerged.

'Alī was asked what guarding oneself before Allah meant, and he replied, 'It means that you obey Him, and you do not disobey.' To obey Allah is, as we said earlier, to obey the physical as well as the spiritual laws. The dominating spiritual law is that the individual must evolve spiritually. The physical laws are easier to discern – if we abuse nature we will pay the price. 'Ali continued by saying, 'That you remember Him and do not forget, and that you are grateful to Him and do not deny Him'.

This state of gratitude is the state of the content heart. The more content the heart is, the more access it has to higher knowledge. A person whose heart is empty and free, a condition which occurs after gratitude, is more likely to succeed in attaining knowledge. Allah has said in the Qur'an that those in gratitude will increase. This process can be rationally observed and tested. Action and reaction are equal and opposite, and therefore the person whose heart is in a state of gratitude must find success and fulfilment to the extent of that gratitude, whether worldly or spiritual. We all know of unjust people who are very successful in the worldly sense, and this success may seem unfair to us at first glance, but if we look deeply, we will discover that they are grateful for what they have. Allah's laws apply to everyone. Though they may be the greatest rascals, their gratitude brings them worldly success. But this success comes with limitations, the most important being that it is restricted to this realm of existence alone, whereas the purpose of creation is to evolve and be ready for life hereafter.

Allah has created out of love and in order to be known. The knowledge of Allah begins by understanding with the intellect the relationship between cause and effect. This knowledge is called unity of action. Then comes the unity of attributes. Here one perceives the attributes in all their diversity and multiplicity, yet knowing that they emanate from but one source. For this knowledge, both head and heart are needed. Lastly comes the knowledge of the unity of essence which can be attained only through a pure heart which is transformed by selfless actions and constant awareness and remembrance of Allah, the ultimate Guide and Merciful One.